D0367693

Running Against the Wind

the transformation of a new age medium
and his warning to the church

Brian Flynn

Second Edition

Lighthouse Trails Publishing
Silverton, Oregon

Running Against the Wind

Library of Congress Cataloging-in-Publication Data

Flynn, Brian, 1958-
  Running against the wind : the transformation of a New Age medium and
his warning to the church / Brian Flynn.— 2nd ed.
    p. cm.
  ISBN 0-9721512-5-7 (softbound : alk. paper)
  1. Christianity and other religions—New Age movement. 2. New Age
movement—Relations—Christianity. 3. Jesus Christ—New Age movement
interpretations. 4. Occultism. 5. Christian converts—Biography. 6. Flynn,
Brian, 1958- I. Title.
BR128.N48F59 2005
261.2'993—dc22
                      2005012814

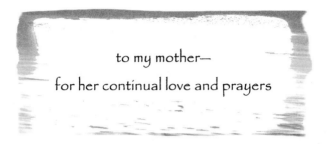

to my mother—

for her continual love and prayers

Acknowledgments

This book could not have been done without the following people:

Renee Beneke for her support and encouragement to write this book and for her professionalism in editing the manuscript.

Bryan and Joan Anderson for their prayers and encouragement in the battle against false teaching in the church.

Pastor Bob DeWaay for his friendship, his biblical knowledge and his instruction on how the church is supposed to lead its flock.

Note: Some of the names of persons and places in this book have been changed to protect privacy.

Contents

Foreword

In 2003, our church (Twin City Fellowship), was asked to host the first *Faith at Risk Conference* in Minneapolis. Lighthouse Trails Publishing had been looking for a location to hold the conference and had actually approached one of the large evangelical churches in the Twin Cities area. When that church learned the conference would be addressing the issue of mysticism in the church, they turned the publishing company down. Through a series of events, Lighthouse Trails heard about Twin City Fellowship and contacted me to see if we would be willing to host the conference.

Controversy was no stranger to our church body. In the 1980s, when Dave Hunt came out with *Seduction of Christianity*, no pastor or church in Minneapolis would risk inviting him to speak. We had read Dave's book and knew his warning to the church was timely and urgent. We called Dave and asked him to speak in our church. Though doing so cost us many friends, we have never regretted inviting Dave to speak.

Thus, when we heard about the contemplative prayer movement through Ray Yungen's book *A Time of Departing* and then through Brian Flynn's testimony, we sensed a similar urgency and were compelled to support these efforts. We agreed to host the *Faith at Risk Conference*, and in so doing had the fortunate opportunity to meet Brian Flynn, one of the conference speakers.

I quickly gained respect for Brian as I witnessed his passion for truth, coupled with a unique ability to communicate and relate his ideas and story to others. He is exceptionally engaging and fearless in the face of a culture within and without the church that resists such warnings. Having spent much of his life in the New Age movement, he brings his message with an urgency that demands a response.

Running Against the Wind is a personal and transparent account of God's sovereign grace, delivering a man who had given himself over to the demonic world of the occult. After Brian became a born-again Christian, much to his shock and dismay, he found within the evangelical church the very practices that had characterized his life in the New Age. His warning is timely and desperately needs to be heard. Christians everywhere are listening to the deceiving voices of the spirit world while naively believing these voices are from God, and they may be closer than you think.

After meeting Brian, it didn't take long to realize he and I shared the same passion for the truth and an equal burden to warn the church about false spirituality. His message of freedom from deception and bondage through the gospel of Jesus Christ resonates with my own calling. God's gracious work in Brian Flynn's life has prepared him to share his story and his warning in a most captivating and compelling manner. I am honored to be his friend and his brother in Christ, and I commend to you his book.

Pastor Bob DeWaay
Twin City Fellowship
Minneapolis, Minnesota

For the **word of God** is living and powerful, and sharper than any two-edged sword, piercing even to the division of soul and spirit, and of joints and marrow, and is a discerner of the thoughts and intents of the heart.—Hebrews 4:12

1

Beginnings

"That's it! We're never going to church again." My father had just made the shocking and unexpected announcement to our family. I was ten years old, and after hearing these words, it felt like the happiest day of my life. I would never have to step inside the boring, monotonous walls of a church again.

* * * * *

Born in Albany, New York, I was the youngest of three children. Dad was Catholic and came from a strong Irish-Scottish background. Mom was an Episcopalian and could trace her family history back to the settling of Troy, New York in the 1600s. Before my dad's parents would allow him to marry Mom, she had to sign a pledge promising to raise their children Catholic, something of which her own mother was not too happy. But Mom loved Dad, and this seemed to be a pledge she was willing to keep. Thus, long before I was even born, family tradition determined my siblings and I would be Catholic.

Dad worked as a printer and was a member of the Printers Union while Mom worked as a secretary for various companies. Neither made a lot of money, and it took both incomes to pay the mortgage and keep bread on the table. Shortly after I was born, my parents bought a house on the outskirts of Albany in what was a new phenomenon called *the suburbs*. My parents paid $17,000 for that house—such a lot of money to spend on a house!

Every Sunday, without fail, my father gathered up my brother, my sister and I, shuffled us to the car, and drove us off to church. For as far back as I can remember Mom never attended church with us. When I was very young, I thought she stayed home because she found church so very monotonous—to this I could totally relate. Later I realized she simply did not believe in the tenets of Catholicism.

As for me, hands down, no question about it—I hated church. I could not stand the thought of getting up early on a weekend, putting on a suit and sitting in church for what seemed like hours, with absolutely nothing to do. At five years old, this was pure torture, and staying awake through the service became a growing challenge. Although I understood the basic beliefs of Christianity and the story of Jesus, I learned more about it from watching television than I did from going to church.

Our parish, St. Thomas Catholic Church, was a traditional looking Catholic church. The building had large heavy doors leading inside to a dimly lit atmosphere. Large stained-glass windows filtered streams of colored daylight across the room. Often, as we entered, Dad would nudge me on the shoulder and whisper, "Stop slouching, son." Quickly I would straighten up, pulling my hands out of my pockets, as we entered this massive building that by its very existence demanded quietness and solemn respect for God.

Since the church offered no separate children's service, we all clambered into a row of seats together, sharing in the misery. My favorite part of the service was the communion—for then I knew we would soon be going home. As I watched each person line up to receive the little cookie and a sip from a cup, my daydreaming began to heighten as I anticipated the freedom I would enjoy all afternoon. Now when I say I watched everyone take communion, I mean *almost* everyone. Our family always sat solemnly gazing upon each person who partook of their weekly wafer and wine, but we never went up to receive ours. Eventually I discovered the requirement for taking communion on Sunday was to make a confession to the priest in one of the small booths on a Saturday. Since Dad never ventured to church on Saturday, he was never allowed to take communion, something I always felt cheated out of, until one Sunday when my sister Bonnie leaned over and whispered, "Those cookies taste terrible—you're lucky you don't have to take them." Somehow that satisfied me, and I never felt deprived again.

St. Thomas had its own grade school, in which all the students had to wear uniforms—ugly purple plaid uniforms. My heart really went out to those kids, who were not able to dress like the rest of us. Partly due to these uniforms, I saw them as goody-good kids who always worried what God thought of them. No doubt about it, public school presented a perfect environment to get away with a lot more mischief—something far more important to me than getting a good education. Since my dad had a deep resentment for Catholic schools and especially for the nuns, he vowed a nun would never teach any child of his. He saw them as cruel disciplinarians, an attitude he developed in his own childhood when corporal punishment was employed to keep children in line—and the nuns were never shy about using it frequently. Since I hated the very idea of attending Catholic school, Dad's own resentments and bitterness worked perfectly to my advantage.

My brother, Bob, was eleven when I was born, and my sister, Bonnie, was eight. Every week they attended church with Dad. In those days, the entire service was in Latin which meant my brother and sister didn't understand a thing said. How could anyone?

When Bob decided to become an altar boy, he also chose to take Latin in high school because he wanted to better understand the service on Sunday. The only formal religious instruction he received that he could understand was during his communion and confirmation classes because they were in English. He learned that communion is the act of confessing one's sins and learning how to accept forgiveness by eating the sacrament (the bread and wine) from the priest. Confirmation was supposed to be the formal commitment that you are a believer in Christ.

This was also at the time, when as a Catholic, eating meat on Fridays was strictly forbidden. And prior to communion, breakfast was not to be eaten. My brother was usually starving by the time we got to church, and the unleavened bread was certainly not a meal. One Friday, Bob forgot the rules, ate a hot dog and thought for sure he was going to go to Hell. My vivid imagination would get the best of me as I pictured my brother standing at the pearly gates shouting, "It was just a hot dog, and it only happened once!" He begs forgiveness, but they still drag him off to Hell.

My first impressions of Christianity came from my father. God was rarely discussed in our household. In fact, the only time religion came up was when we went to church on Sunday, or when someone died, or when Dad jumped up and shouted, "Jesus, Mary and Joseph," when Notre Dame fumbled the football—other than those times, our home, our conversations, and our thoughts never drifted into a realm that included God.

When I attended my communion classes, I asked the nun what Jesus' middle name was. She gave me an odd look and answered that he didn't have one. I told her my dad often refers to Jesus as Jesus "H" Christ. "What does the 'H' stand for?" I asked. As the nun just stood there and glared at me, I suddenly knew what my dad meant when he said a nun could instill dreadful fear with just one look.

In Catholic tradition, first communion had to be made before the age of six. I wasn't aware at the time that I was two years late when I attended communion classes until I realized I was the only fourth grader in a class of second graders. I don't think most of my classmates noticed, since I didn't look much older than they. I was the shortest and skinniest kid in my class, thus providing ample entertainment for my friends as they would often pick me up to see how light I was. Under- weighing everyone by quite a bit, I could never fight back physically, so I developed a fast, razor sharp wit I used to cut the other guy down to size. It was the only weapon I had.

As the communion class began, the nun asked if we were all part of God's family. Thinking about that for a moment, I reasoned to myself, *God has a big family up there already, so the answer must be no.* My hand shot up as I blurted out an emphatic, "No!" The nun shot me one of those *looks* again.

Then with a bit of a twist to her smile, the Sister asked the class, "Does Brian have the right answer?"

"No!" they all sang in unison.

"What *is* the right answer?" she asked, as I began to realize my blunder. Feeling my face burn with embarrassment, I shrank in my seat while the class continued with their jaunting and laughing.

"Yes, we are," they shouted. Although I managed to pass the class and make my communion, that class was the first and last formal education I received about the Bible or the resurrection during my childhood.

Freedom At Last

One sunny Sunday morning, I awoke later than usual and immediately began wondering what I'd be forced to wear. Climbing down the stairs, I could smell the aroma of toasted bread and fried eggs. If it wasn't for the fact we had to go to church, it would have been a perfect morning. Mom and Dad were sitting at the dining room table already, and I realized I must have slept in, as they were finished eating. My brother and sister were just about to get up and leave the table, Mom sipped on her coffee, and Dad, in his usual after-breakfast-pose, was behind the newspaper. The headline read: *Did Sirhan Sirhan Act Alone?*

As I quietly slipped into my chair, Dad put down the newspaper and announced, "Don't get dressed for church." I threw a quick glance at my dad.

"Why?" I asked rather incredulously as I pulled toast off a nearby plate.

"We're not going," he replied.

"Why, Dad," I asked?

"Because I said so." His tone demanded silence.

He raised the newspaper again and went back to reading. When my dad gave his *because-I-said-so* answer that meant no more questions. But I could hardly believe my ears and finally, after several agonizing moments, my curiosity got the best of me. I had to press further. "Do you really mean it, Dad? No more church?" I further questioned.

He peered over the newspaper and said, "I have decided we are *never* going to church again."

Was he serious? My heart danced with glee inside. It had only been a few days since my tenth birthday—this was like an additional bonus gift. *Never again*, I thought. No more waking up early. No more wearing a tie. No more boring sermons to listen to. No more sitting behind old men in church who smelled like last night's beer. Inside I was screaming, *Yahoo!!* I fought back my smile, afraid if I looked too happy, he'd quickly change his mind. "Never again, but why Dad?"

I could sense he did not want to discuss the subject, but he reluctantly added, "Because the church is getting too modern. They now have *folk masses* with people playing guitar on the altar. It's a disgrace, and I am through with it all."

That was it, it was over. No more church ever again. Dad was serious, and he kept his word. From that day on, my father never went to church again—for the remainder of his life! As for me, years would pass before I ever stepped foot inside another church.

A few days prior to all this, an incident had taken place that I soon wondered if it was connected. Two nuns came to our house to inquire of my father why I was not attending my confirmation classes. My father told them what he really thought about the church—the disgrace of folk masses, non-ordained people speaking on the pulpit, the mass no longer given in Latin and his general disgust with the entire Catholic Church. Vatican II had been implemented just a few years earlier and the changes in the church were starting to take hold—my father did not accept or like any of them. Through the walls, I heard raised voices, a door slamming, and then the nuns were gone. After telling them what he thought, he threw them out of the house. A few days later, at the breakfast table, Dad made his earth-shattering announcement.

Many years later, when I was grown, Dad lay on his deathbed after several recurrences of cancer. He had never gone back to church, and I'm not sure if he ever knew what it meant to be a Christian. He turned his back on the church because he felt it had turned its back on the traditions, rituals and practices that had always been followed. Did he know before he died that these rituals and practices could not bring anyone into God' presence but rather that it comes from repentance of sins and faith in Jesus Christ? Eventually my father succumbed to the disease that had chased him for seven years. He remained stubborn until the end. When asked if he would like his last communion and his last rites to be performed by a priest, he refused. He died minutes later holding onto my mother's hand.

The Downward Spiral

When I was fourteen, I read about Tarot cards and how they were used to *tell the future*. The Tarot cards are shuffled and placed in specific arrangements; the order and position they land in is considered fortuitous, predicting future events or giving perspective on what is going to happen in an individual's life. Not only does each card have a different meaning, but if placed upside down it has the opposite meaning. There are 78 cards in a deck, 22 in the major arcana and 56 in the minor arcana. The major arcana cards most often used, are identified as the Fool, the Magician, the High Priestess, the Empress, the Emperor, the Hierophant, the Lovers, the Chariot, Strength, the Hermit, the Wheel of Fortune, Justice, the Hanged Man, Death, Temperance, the Devil, the Tower, the Star, the Moon, the Sun, Judgment, and the World. The four suits of the minor arcana are Wands, Swords, Cups, and the Pentacles.

The moment I heard about Tarot cards, I knew I had to have them. Not having enough money of my own, Mom agreed to get me the cards and the instruction booklet that went with them. Every night after that, I sat in my room and read with absolute interest, devouring each word of the instructions. At the book's suggestion, I placed the deck of cards under my pillow before I went to sleep so the cards would become more familiar to me. Supposedly, the more frequently the cards were handled the more accurate the readings would be. I did that for several nights until my neck became so sore from laying on them I finally had to stop. I was hoping that just keeping them next to me in bed would have the same effect.

In order to memorize the countless meanings of each card and placing, I carried the book with me everywhere I went. At school, I began performing readings for my friends in the cafeteria at lunch time. The best thing about performing the readings was the attention I got from girls—one of the most important things to a fourteen-year-old boy.

Performing the readings was great fun, and occasionally I got something right. But, of course, there was always someone in the crowd eager to ruin the fun. One of the most *prudish* girls in school, Constance, would stand behind everyone, watching, and just at the wrong moment, with her arms folded defiantly she would start scoffing at everything I said during a reading.

"Brian, my mom said Tarot cards are the devil's work, and you shouldn't be doing that!" she cried out.

"Go away Constance; no one cares what you think," I responded. "You Christians are always so judgmental and scared of everything."

"I am not scared," she retorted, "but you don't know what you are involved in. Something bad is going to happen, and you are going to go to Hell!"

My friends laughed at her reprimanding reaction. Although I laughed too, her words haunted me at times, and I tried reassuring myself that nothing bad would ever happen to me as a result of reading Tarot cards, proving of course that Christians were wrong—an opinion I cherished and one that grew stronger with each passing year.

My two best friends in high school were Ben and Jake. Ben and I spent a lot of our time drinking, getting high and talking about girls. Our buddy Jake didn't go along with our drinking and getting high but was one of the best guitar players in school. Jake's family, devout Catholics, attended church every Sunday. His mother knew my family had a very lax attitude about the church and religion in general, and she didn't like me very much. Somehow she believed I would be a negative influence on Jake—she couldn't have been more right. Ben and I finally convinced Jake to get drunk and start smoking weed. But even with all our corrupting influence, Jake still took the whole religion thing very seriously. Many times I raced over to

Jake's house after school for guitar lessons only to find the priest from his church at the house. The family liked this priest so much they invited him to birthdays, dinner parties, and other family events, and he always showed up.

Then one afternoon, after my guitar lesson, Jake invited Ben and me to go for pizza with a few of his friends and two of the priests who were over visiting his mom. When we arrived at the pizza parlor, the two priests were sitting around the table with our friends, and they had started drinking—something I had never seen a priest do before. They ordered Vodka tonics and were on their second round when we sat down. Sitting next to one of the priests, I blurted out, "I didn't know priests could drink!" He laughed but didn't respond to my comment. These priests were unlike any I had ever met before. Soon, it became obvious they were getting pretty drunk as they plunged into telling a string of dirty jokes. *These guys are pretty cool,* I thought to myself. *Sure not like the old stuffed priests I used to know.*

As the late afternoon turned into early evening, whenever the priest sitting next to me told a joke or laughed he placed a hand on my back or rubbed my shoulder or neck. Although it seemed a little unusual, I didn't think much of it at the time. Soon though this friendly priest had his arm around my shoulder and left it there. I was puzzled by this, but after all, he was a priest and was just being friendly—until he began dropping his hand down my back and started pulling up my shirt. Shocked and confused, I froze. I didn't know what to do. He then lifted my shirt up and started putting his hand down the back of my pants. I couldn't believe what was happening. I didn't want to say anything because I knew Jake would have been very upset. Instead, I jumped up and grabbed Ben while saying under my breath, "Follow me now!" He saw the twisted look on my face and hurried after me. As we burst into the men's room, Ben let out a yelp, "What's wrong?"

"That priest is putting his hand in my pants!"

"What!" he nearly shouted.

"I have to get out of here. I am not sitting next to that freak again," I said as I tucked my shirt back into my pants. "Don't tell

Jake—this is one of his favorite priests."

"Don't tell me what?" Jake said as he came around the corner. "Why did you guys suddenly leave the table?"

At that moment I couldn't hold back, even for the sake of Jake's feelings. "Your favorite priest is putting his hand down my pants."

"No way, he would never do that," Jake adamantly insisted.

"He did! He must be gay, and I'm not going back to that table! C'mon Ben, let's get out of here," I retorted. We left Jake in the restaurant looking pretty stunned.

Jake and I never spoke about it again. In fact, I don't think he wanted to be reminded of the incident. He did mention it to Ben once saying he thought I was wrong and that I misinterpreted the circumstance. This incident was just another reminder of what frauds I believed Christians were. I saw them as people who run around telling everyone how perfect they are and how everyone should be just like them. Then they begin their "you're going to Hell" line. As far as I was concerned, they were all liars and hypocrites.

Throughout high school, one of my goals was to get good enough grades to qualify for the Air Force Academy. My brother was in the Air Force as a recruiter, and my sister joined the Air Force Reserve. The men in my family had all served in the military with my father being a Navy man during World War II. My grandfather on my mother's side had served in the Marines in World War I and the Army in World War II. He won the French Croix Deguerre (the French Medal of Honor) for saving several men in the battle of Belleau Woods in France during World War I. Due to my lack of focus and being more concerned with partying, my grades would not allow me to qualify for the academy. My parents had little money for me to go to college, so I decided to join the Air Force and qualify for college tuition through the GI Bill. In the year of America's bicentennial, I graduated from high school and two weeks later left home to join the Air Force.

In the last years of my grandfather's life, he lost a leg due to an infection. I found it disturbing to see a man I admired so much reduced to being pushed around in a wheelchair by my grandmother. *Papa*, as we affectionately called my grandfather, seldom went to church, but in the last summer of his life he spent many afternoons with the local pastor. At the time, I couldn't understand that at all. Looking back now, I'm sure he knew his time was growing short, and he would soon be answering to God for his life and his need for atonement for his sins. As so many have, he had been deceived by a false sense of longevity, putting off what he always figured he could get around to later. Suddenly, he realized his last moments on this earth were coming to an end.

But for me at eighteen, life was just beginning. I was through with high school, religion was not something I had to worry about, and I could see only good things for my future. Little did I know at the time, life would take me in a direction I never would have imagined.

2

Dark Side of the Moon

"Hey rainbows, down in front." Rainbow was the nickname used for guys new to basic training who had not yet received their uniforms.

Matthew, a fellow Air Force trainee, and I had just arrived at the Air Force church service. Matthew looked angry and shot back, "This is church—not the barracks!"

The hecklers laughed and yelled even louder, "Sit down and shut up rainbow!" Matthew was from Oregon and a real *Bible thumper* who took his faith very seriously. Every night before we fell exhausted into our beds, Matthew dropped to his knees and prayed. It was also the first thing he did when he awoke. While the rest of us hurried to make our beds before first inspection, he was down on his knees praying. *What a strict life,* I thought. *And for what?*

My basic training in the Air Force began in San Antonio, Texas. When the Air Force asked me what religion I was, I told them "Catholic," which seemed as good an answer as any. Church services were mandatory for all, and few protested this opportunity to get away from the barracks, if only for a short while. And since I said Catholic, it was the Catholic Church I was off to, along with about twenty other guys.

When we arrived at church that first Sunday, several hundred people were already seated. As we found places to sit, I studied the pulpit—an organ, a bass and a set of drums filled the spaces of the stage. I had never seen instruments, other than the guitar my father protested against, on a pulpit before. Three black musicians walked up as the service began and started to play. The drummer began laying down a hard funk backbeat while the bass player started bass popping. Soon, the parishioners started clapping and getting into the music. This music was like nothing I had ever heard before in church. It was great! The choir kicked in with a gospel version of the hymn, *Amazing Grace.* Three black women sitting in front of us stood up and started waving their hands above their heads, while clapping and singing. When the majority of the congregation suddenly stood up, I jumped up too and joined them, clapping and singing along. After five days of being told to keep quiet while worrying about everything we said and did, it felt great to let loose a little. As I swayed to the rhythm of the beat, I looked down at Matthew who was frozen in his seat—he looked horrified! I had a feeling this was *not* his idea of church.

Matthew never said a word throughout the entire service. Later as we walked back to our barracks, he finally broke the silence, "That wasn't church, that was a disgrace! I have never witnessed such a display in my life. People shouting and dancing during the service?"

"Oh man, I loved it!" I quickly returned. "It was fun." Shaking his head, he gave me a disgusted look.

"You won't catch me back there again. I'd rather sit in the barracks by myself than go through that again." He kept his word. The following Sunday he stayed behind, alone, in his barracks. I couldn't understand his attitude. *Why does being a Christian have to be such a drag? When are you ever able to have some fun?* I was convinced I would never be able to live the rigid lifestyle in which Matthew's faith insisted.

Basic Training finally ended, and from there I was sent to technical training school in Biloxi, Mississippi. I had wanted to get involved in Air Traffic Control for Air Defense, but once I got to the school, I realized my job would involve sitting in front of a radarscope watching little green blips rather than really controlling aircraft. Not exactly what I had in mind!

I also did not anticipate running into God and religion everywhere I went. As hard as I tried to steer in the absolute opposite direction, I couldn't avoid the collision. One of the guys in my classes, Alan, proved to be just such a reminder. He was from Georgia and had plans to become an Air Force chaplain. Alan amazed me with how many verses from the Bible he could quote off the top of his head. I had to admit—it was rather impressive.

And then came Carl. Alan and I met Carl who was 6'6" and 250 pounds of raw muscle but unfortunately not the sharpest knife in the drawer. He was late for class the first three times because he couldn't remember the number of the room where we met.

Although Carl seemed slow in most respects, he had an incredible memory for dirty jokes. At lunch he could go on telling one joke after another without missing a beat. Most of us found him hilarious. Carl especially liked it when Alan sat with us and without fail, he always reserved the dirtiest jokes to tell in front of Alan. "There's nothing as enjoyable as tweaking Christians," Carl sneered often to me. He thought people like Alan were weak. "And I sure don't need anyone telling me God wants to take care of me—I can take care of myself."

Carl had his reasons for this bitterness. His father raised Carl and his two younger sisters in a strict Catholic manner, attending church every Sunday, taking communion, and making confession. When Carl turned twelve, his father had an affair and finally left his mother for another woman. After this, Carl became the man of the house, taking care of his mother and sisters. Carl's mother was convinced that if she prayed hard enough her husband would return. Alas, he never did, and in sadness and despair, Carl watched his mother fall apart under the burden of being abandoned and having to support the family alone. From then on, Carl saw prayer as a waste of time. He decided if God wouldn't listen to someone as good as his mother, why would He listen to anyone else.

Everyday at lunch seemed to be a repeat of the previous day— Carl told his dirty jokes, and Alan sat silently, pretending not to hear. Carl especially loved to tell of his sexual conquests, needling Alan constantly about sex and his lack of experience. Alan had shared with us how he was engaged and was going to wait until marriage before having sex, which Carl thought was ridiculous. Although I agreed with Carl, it seemed inappropriate to make fun of a minister, especially about sex. It was obvious this made Alan angry and probably disheartened, but he never responded to anything Carl had to say.

During the third week of class, our first-aid instructor selected Alan to be the first to perform mouth-to-mouth resuscitation on the practice dummy, which just happened to be a female. Alan looked noticeably uncomfortable. As he bent over to begin, Carl blurted out, "I'll bet this is the first time you've gotten this close to a woman, right Alan?" The whole class erupted in laughter. Alan looked embarrassed but said nothing. When the class ended, Alan approached Carl and said he wanted to talk to him after class. Carl shrugged his shoulders and said, "Sure."

The next day at lunch Carl was very quiet. While we all talked about class and the latest news, Carl said almost nothing. Alan read a letter from his fiancee, and not once did Carl chime in with something to chide Alan about. After class I walked back with Alan and asked what happened the night before between him and Carl. Alan didn't give me many details out of respect for Carl, but he did say Carl was angry with God, not at him. "Is Carl a Christian now?" I asked.

"No," Alan answered, "but he understands a lot more about God than he did before." Whatever Alan had said to him made a lasting impression. The remaining two weeks in class Carl did not tell one dirty joke—at least not when Alan was around.

Blind Faith

Although my stay in Biloxi lasted only eight weeks I made some close friends before I left. One of them, a tall, thin guy named Bennett, was getting married soon and invited me to his wedding in Georgia. He said we could drive the ten hours to get there, but I would have to take the bus back after the wedding. Honored he would invite me, I immediately agreed to go. The wedding turned out to be great, and his parents and friends showered me with good ol' Southern hospitality.

The bus trip back to Mississippi was rather uneventful until we stopped in a small town in Alabama. A man wearing an Air Force uniform and the customary short hair cut got on the bus and took the seat next to me. As the bus rolled out onto the highway, John introduced himself and said he was going to be an Air Force Chaplain and that he too was from the Biloxi Air Force Base.

With a long ride ahead of us, John and I passed the time talking about family, the Air Force and eventually, of course, the conversation headed down that all-too-familiar road of God and faith. When he asked me if I was a Christian, I gave him my favorite, smart-aleck reply, "I'm a Catholic agnostic," ending the statement with a hearty laugh. Not finding my sarcasm funny at all, he asked, "What does *that* mean?"

"I was born a Catholic—I believe there is a God—but I really don't know who He is nor do I think anyone knows that."

"Do you want to know?" he asked.

"Listen," I snapped. "Don't bother preaching to me—I don't believe anyone knows the truth. It's up to each person to decide what is true and what is not. The Bible was written by so many different people so long ago no one really knows what happened back then."

"You need to look past the inconsistencies of the Bible," he replied with obvious irritation. "Just feel it in your heart."

I asked him several questions regarding the veracity of the Bible, and he seemed stumped by all of them. "If you just accept it as the truth, you would know it's the truth."

As the bus pulled into the base I argued, "So, in other words, it's all blind faith?" He got up from his seat to retrieve his bag in the overhead bin and then sat back down.

"Brian," he continued. "If you don't repent from this life you're leading, you are going to go to Hell. You either have to decide to become a Christian, or you are just lost!" He got up from his seat, turned to me, and in an angry tone said, "You need to get down on your knees tonight and beg that the Lord forgives you."

Although his words infuriated me, I also felt scared. *Maybe I will go to Hell. Maybe I am a bad person.* That night when I returned to my room, I got down on my knees and prayed to God to forgive me. However, waking the next morning, I felt no difference. My life was the same; I was the same. Nothing had changed, and I dismissed the whole thing. *I'm a good person,* I told myself, *and it isn't necessary to be a Christian. I've let some angry pastor who thinks everyone should be like him make me feel guilty about my life.* I just could not accept a religion based on blind faith. As I headed out the door of the dorms, I pulled my jacket closer around my neck. A north wind blew through the trees and then whistled past my ears. I felt a sense of confidence once more that religion and I just didn't mix. *I'm getting along just fine without that garbage.*

My first assignment in the Air Force after basic training was at the Duluth Air Force Base. My hopes of getting out and seeing the world through the Air Force were being dashed to the ground. Mississippi, Duluth … not exactly what I had in mind. Assigned in Duluth to the 23rd Air Defense Division, my job was to help defend the United States from air attack, guiding fighter aircraft to intercept any unknown aircraft entering the United States. It sounded pretty impressive, but most of the time we guided F-106s and F-4s to play bump heads inside airspace to practice intercepts. In between those practice missions, I, along with the others in the crew, watched green blips moving across the screen from Lake Erie to Winnipeg—not exactly the intrigue and adventure I had hoped for.

Growing up watching the Vietnam war on television and Richard Nixon resigning in disgrace, changed our generation. *America, love it or leave it* was an attitude most of my generation did not subscribe to. Instead, we liked partying, smoking weed and growing our hair long. This, of course, did not line up with the Air Force rules of acceptance. Rather than see this kind of sheer defiance, they expected obedience to authority, short hair and an absolute *no* to drugs. Along with several others, I managed to ignore every one of those rules. It wasn't that we weren't patriotic or didn't believe in defending America— we just had a problem with obeying authority without question. Drugs and getting high was the ultimate act of defiant behavior. The penalty for getting caught, however, was rather costly—demotion, which meant less of a paycheck or even possibly a dishonorable discharge. Anything other than an honorable discharge would have been a disgrace in my family. Yet none of that stopped me.

Although I never took any drugs while on duty, I managed to get high six out of the seven days in any given week. Some of the guys were high all the time, on and off duty. Often they sat on the roof of the Strategic Air Defense building on their breaks and smoked, always making sure they used eye drops before coming back down. Why no one ever noticed the smell on them was a mystery to me.

One day my buddy, Dan, told me some of the guys were forming a band—did I want to join? I played guitar in high school, but I hardly considered myself good enough to play in a band. "Actually," Dan began, "we don't need a guitar player, we need a bass player."

"I've never played bass before, but I'll sure give it a try."

"I'll put it this way," he replied. "If you buy a bass you're in the band. Welcome to rock 'n' roll."

As a band, we did everything we could to become good players. We listened to songs together trying to figure out our parts and went to rock clubs across the bay in Superior, Wisconsin to watch, listen and learn how to play from the best bands in the area. The best club in town at that time was The Cove, which brought in top hard-rock bands in the upper Midwest. Often, we hung out after the club closed, getting high with the guys in the band and talking into the wee hours of the morning about music.

As with all good things that come to an end, the owner of The Cove announced they were going to gut the place and turn it into a disco—no more bands! Years after the disco era had waned everywhere else, it had finally infiltrated its way into the small town of Superior. The Cove's dark atmosphere and powerful sound system, where great rock 'n' roll was performed, were replaced by a plastic-lighted dance floor so guys wearing polyester shirts could do *the Hustle*. What a disgrace!

The singer in our band, Pat, was an avid fan of Bob Dylan *and* of smoking weed. We spent many nights sitting and listening to Dylan and taking bong hits. It amazes me to this day we never got caught. On occasion, the officers on base brought dogs in the dorm looking for drugs. Luckily, each time an inspection took place we had advance warning before it happened. We would rush to clean out everything in our rooms and then sprinkle pepper in our doorways to make the dogs sneeze and throw them off scent.

My friends and I caused some trouble on base, and we were not well thought of. In 1977, having short hair was not considered cool. Thus there was no way we could play in a hard-rock band, be cool, and have short hair all at the same time. Finally, we figured out a way to beat the regulations. Air Force rules stated that hair must be *groomed* above the ears. Groomed, not cut. We started plastering our long hair above our ears with Dippity Du while on duty, then washed it out when we were off duty. We patted ourselves on the back for coming up with such an ingenious plan, but the officers were furious that we had managed to out-maneuver the Air Force regulations. Our First Sergeant took a lot of flack on our behalf. The only reason he defended us at all was because of our exemplary record on the job. Our team had been chosen to take the lead when any difficult training or mission was scheduled.

Stepping Toward Darkness

I had become totally hooked on rock 'n' roll and being a musician. The more I played with the band, the less I wanted to remain in the Air Force. I began to resent every rule and regulation I had to follow. My answer to this growing resentment was easy—getting high as often as I could. One night after practice with the band, Pat asked me if I had ever dropped acid before. I confessed that the closest I had come to an LSD trip was witnessing my older sister and her friends dropping acid when I was ten years old. My sister hung out with guys from a band, and they got high quite often. I thought they were hilarious to watch after they did LSD. You could keep them entertained for hours by giving them a rubber band. They would stretch it between their fingers and laugh hysterically like it was a new and fascinating toy. I would purposely wave my hand in front of their faces so they could watch the trails that followed behind, or I'd jump out from behind a chair to freak them out. When Pat suggested I try LSD, although I was hesitant, I felt I was long overdue in trying this drug—so without giving it too much thought, I agreed to take a ride on the psychedelic train of illusion.

Pat planned my first LSD trip the way someone plans an afternoon picnic on a sunny hillside. One Saturday, Pat brought over the little purple pills. Handing one to me and taking one himself, we began our journey. Sitting back, drinking beer and listening to music, I began experiencing a slight feeling of euphoria—then it began to build into a very happy energetic high. We started dancing around the room drinking, singing and at times laughing uncontrollably.

I kept on asking as each hour passed whether we had reached the *peak* yet. Pat yelled above the music, "No way man, we have a long way to go!" The peak, I was told, was a tremendous feeling of euphoria followed by a long descent with hallucinations, bright colors and distortions of every kind. Hours later I experienced the *peak*—a strange and yet exhilarating experience. As I felt like I was floating, the music moved me and took me on a psychedelic journey. When I saw Pat's telephone melt down the side of his nightstand forming a puddle on the floor, I just laughed. Fortunately, Pat had prepared me for these odd visions, or I might have really freaked out.

With each passing hour, I became more reflective, and my senses seemed very acute. We listened to Pink Floyd's *Dark Side of the Moon,* and as we listened, the subliminal tracks that I had always tried to hear but never could became as clear as day.

The long trip ended the following morning, and I went back to my room to sleep it off. Pat told me this trip would forever change the way I looked at life and reality. He was right. I felt I experienced something beyond the visible, tangible every day world. I knew I had just experienced another level of consciousness, another world beyond the five senses and another way to look at things. Realizing the mind had so much more potential than I had originally thought,

I felt sure LSD provided a way to discover this potential. I took several more LSD trips while in the Air Force, but later when my service came to an end, I came to the conclusion that dropping LSD gave me no lasting sense of peace or satisfaction. It often brought me to what seemed the brink of true reality but would always disappoint. When I left the service, I left LSD behind with it.

Eventually, I received transfer papers that read, "Fort Yukon, Alaska." I stared at the transfer papers in disbelief. When I joined the Air Force, I saw it as my vehicle to see the world and experience great adventure. With Mississippi and Duluth behind me, Alaska before me, it didn't look like that was going to happen. But with no choice in the matter, I packed my bags and headed for the airport, off to the Alaskan wilderness.

After flying into Fairbanks International Airport, I boarded a small six-passenger plane to make the rest of the trip. The scenery was spectacular and later as we approached Fort Yukon, I could understand why there were only two ways in, by plane and by riverboat—the small range of mountains surrounding Fort Yukon made it impassable for any ground vehicle no matter what time of the year it was. The United States Air Force was depositing me in the middle of nowhere!

The plane shot across the Yukon River, touching down on a dirt runway. The copilot turned and said, "This is Fort Yukon, bud, have fun." He laughed and then added, "I hope you like drunken Indians, because there's plenty of em' here." I didn't say anything as I reached to get my bag. I had heard rumors about the Indians but refused to give into the stereotype that all of them were drunks.

In Fort Yukon, only the hardcore residents stayed throughout the winter, bringing the summer population of one thousand down to a mere 400 in the winter. The citizens of Fort Yukon were 98 percent Athebaskin Indian and 2 percent white.

A stern-looking man in uniform approached me and said, "Airman Flynn?"

"Yes sir," I replied.

"I'm Sergeant Baxter. I'm here to take you to the base." He

looked at my ears, checking to see if my hair was cut properly.

I hopped in the back of his Datsun truck, and we headed towards the base. As we drove through town an unfamiliar fragrance permeated the air. I later discovered it was the smell of drying Moose skin, of which several residents made moccasins. The young people were no longer learning this skill since most of them wore sneakers like most other American kids. Only the older residents clung to the traditions of the past.

The Indian children playing in the street all had such pretty faces. I waved to a cute little girl standing on the corner. She looked no more than seven years old. As I waved, her face turned from a smile to a grimace, and she gave me the finger—so much for the cute kids. The Air Force guys and white people in general were not very popular in Fort Yukon. And suddenly I realized that for the first time in my life, I was a minority.

Life in the Yukon

On my first night, a fellow named Mike took me into town to drink and party with a few of the Indian guys he knew. When we arrived at the party, everyone was already pretty drunk.

I felt strangely out of place, not knowing anyone and not sure who liked me or who hated me. I stuck close to Mike and any of the Indian guys he talked to. One of the guys, a tall Indian with long hair said to Mike, "Ready to race, Vonneclid?"

"I'm ready when you are," he replied. Mike took a big shot of whiskey and headed towards his truck.

Edward, the tall guy, said, "Hey, we'll take your new guy in the truck with us. Edward grabbed me and said, "Get in the truck." I wasn't sure what was going to happen, but to avoid appearing wimpy, I followed him to the truck.

I hopped in and was suddenly sandwiched between Edward who was driving and a fellow named Samuel on my right. My mind began to imagine the worst as I realized, while squeezed in between two big, drunk Indians I had never met, we were about to race ... backwards. Edward turned to me and said, "We need to drink a little more to make it fun." He pulled out a bottle of Everclear and took a big gulp. Then he passed it to me and said, "You gotta have some too Vonneclid." I pretended to gulp some down but mostly just wet my tongue with it instead. My tongue turned numb on contact.

"It's backward truck racing time!" Mike yelled from the other truck. Before I knew it, we were racing down a hill side-by-side going backwards. A dense cloud of dust surrounded us as we barreled down the road. I could hear Mike screaming as we went faster and faster. Edward shouted to Samuel, "The Vonneclid looks scared."

Samuel laughed and said, "All white guys are scared."

"I didn't think it was possible to go this fast in reverse gear," I shouted above the roar of the engine.

Edward laughed and said, "What gear? I'm not in reverse. We are coasting, man."

"Edward, turn, man, turn; the turn is coming up!" Samuel shouted. He grabbed the wheel, and we spun around and watched as Mike went by barely missing us by inches as he plunged over the embankment into a ditch. Mike's truck tipped over as it slid over the embankment and came to rest leaning on its side.

We jumped out of the truck and ran toward the ditch. As we reached the embankment, Mike crawled out of the truck, laughing hysterically.

"Are you all right?" I asked him, staring in disbelief.

"Yeah, no problem man," he replied with a grin.

As I slid down to the truck, I said in a low voice to Mike, "That was scary."

"Just another night on the Yukon," he replied. "You'll have all sorts of fun here if you make friends with the townies."

"Looks like you're right about that," I said, just glad we were all still alive.

The experience of living in a self-contained community surrounded by the incredible beauty of the wilderness was filled with stress and loneliness on one side and the enrichment of solitude on the other.

Fort Yukon Air Force Station was a small radar installation monitoring the eastern side of Alaska. We were on constant lookout for the possibility of attack. Most of the time, we sat and watched major airliners arcing their way towards Japan, China or South Korea. I thought many times about the people in those planes flying to exciting destinations, living interesting lives, as I sat watching them cross my screen and disappear. Our own work was tedious, non-rewarding and dull. The only excitement was the occasional mission simulation when we played war and shot down the *bad guys*.

I spent most of my free time drinking beer, getting high on occasion and going to town to meet the locals. One afternoon I met a guy named Bill Black. He was a blues guitar player who had a band, and it just so happened they were looking for a bass player. I was in luck—in the middle of Nowhere, America I found a band to join.

After one of the gigs in town, I met the drummer's sister, Sara. She was sweet and friendly, and we seemed to hit it off right away. However, she swore she would never date a white man, and though I could tell she liked me, she refused to acknowledge it. She and many of her friends held a strong resentment for white people and especially the Air Force guys. I could understand their distrust of the Air Force personnel since most of them just wanted to take a woman to bed and then leave when their time at the post had ended.

Sara's resentment for white people stemmed also from her attendance at the Bureau of Indian Affairs schools as a teenager. The BIA schools employed harsh corporal punishment for any infraction. All the students were Indian, and all the teachers were white. Beatings were common for students who were late for class or who talked out of turn. The white teachers treated all of them like they were savages that needed to be beaten to be kept in line. Witnessing these things formed Sara's views and deepened her resentment. Over time, however, she learned my intentions were honorable, and she gradually lowered her defenses. It wasn't long before we were considered a couple.

One morning, while sitting in the cafeteria, Sergeant Baxter approached me. Never one to mince words, he asked, "Are you a Catholic, Flynn?"

"Well, I consider myself a Catholic agnostic," I said with a laugh.
"No wise remarks—just answer the question," he barked.
"Yes, I am, but I don't practice it," I answered.
"Good," he replied. "A priest is here, and he wants to meet with each Catholic individually. You are to meet with him at 1400 hours." He turned on his heel before I could say anything further.

At 1400 hours, I walked into a small office to wait for the priest. Soon a tall man of about 35 years of age walked into the room. "You're Airman Flynn, is that right?" he asked without looking up from the notepad he held.

"Yes sir," I replied.

"No need for 'yes sirs' with me; just call me Father Donovan," he urged.

"And you can call me Brian," I returned. I expected an older man since all the priests I had ever met were well over sixty.

He sat down and without further ado began: "Brian, are you a Christian? Where are you with God? Do you have a relationship with our Lord Jesus Christ?" He shot these questions to me without pausing between them.

"Well, to be honest, I don't like the church *or* religion," I answered with all the confidence I could muster up. *I'm not going to let this guy think I'm interested in all this.* "I believe in God, but I don't believe one religion is any better or more right than the other. I honestly don't think it makes a difference whether someone is Catholic, Buddhist or a Hindu for that matter."

Father Donovan looked surprised and somewhat dismayed by my answer. "Brian, you put down in your file you are a Catholic. Why?"

Shrugging my shoulders, I then began with my usual tirade. "Listen, if you are here to convince me to become a true Catholic, you are wasting your time. All the Catholics I knew growing up showed up to church on Sunday, acting proper and good, and then would go right back to drinking and partying the rest of the week. It is all a fraud if you ask me. They are all hypocrites."

Father Donovan responded rather defensively, "We are not all like that Brian. All of us battle sin and the sin around us."

"Sin is just a word you use to make people feel guilty," I replied, "There is no sin, and I am not a sinner. I am a good person. Organized religion is about power and money. You make people feel guilty if they don't contribute enough money to the church or if they don't show up to church often enough."

Father Donovan's expression went from one of dismay to shock. He acted as though no one had ever challenged him like this before. I went on for another ten minutes telling him all the problems I had with the Catholic Church, the Bible, and the whole Christian thing. It felt good putting him on the spot and watching him squirm. I was surprised at how good I had gotten at leaving these religious guys with little defense. But after all, I now had years of experience. I guess I was taking revenge for all the garbage I took from Christians who told me I was going to Hell. *They can all go to Hell as far as I am concerned,* I thought to myself at that moment.

"I don't think you understand the Church, Brian," he said rather timidly. "There are repercussions for ignoring God."

"I'll take my chances Father." I stood up to leave the room. He looked so disturbed. For a moment I felt a little guilty. *Maybe I was a little harsh,* I thought. *After all he is a Father. Maybe I should have gone a little easier on the poor guy.* I stopped in front of the door and said, "Listen Father, don't worry—I'll be fine. Some people can be religious and get into all that stuff, but it's just not for me, okay?"

"I will pray for you my son." I turned and walked out leaving him staring bewildered down at his notepad.

Later that night, I thought about how I had reacted and the things I said to him. I was amazed how little he said to defend himself or his religion. I was expecting him to take me on and challenge me, but he didn't. I thought a priest would have some better responses, but like many other religious people I had met, they seldom had any good answers to my questions.

Time moved swiftly, and my time at Fort Yukon soon neared an end. I had survived the frigid winters, with temperatures dropping as low as 83 degrees below zero, and the hangovers from the non-stop beer drinking that went on nearly every night. I had fallen for Sara and invited her to come to live with me in Minneapolis.

Before I left, the townspeople who had become my friends arranged a birthday party for me. Several of my bandmates, Air Force buddies and all my Indian friends came out to wish me well. One of the elder women in the community gave me a gift—a pair of handmade moose skin moccasins. The tops were adorned with beautiful hand-woven beadwork. The smell of moose skin was the first scent I experienced when I arrived in Fort Yukon. This gift of kindness tugged at my heart, and I knew I would miss this community.

Over the years, many misunderstandings, prejudices and fights had occurred between the townspeople and the Air Force people. Through my relationship with Sara, and by playing in the band, I had the opportunity to explain some things, smooth over past disagreements and help resolve certain problems that had existed. I felt honored to be part of this process, and the recognition I was given that night at the party meant so much to me.

As I was eating a piece of cake, a large Indian man approached me. In the entire time I lived there, this particular man had never spoken to me. His name was Nathan, and rumors had spread that he knifed one of the Air Force men a few months before I had arrived. He hated white people and especially guys from the base. As he came nearer, I stood still and waited for him to pass by. Instead, he stopped in front of me and said, "A birthday party for a white guy." He shook his head in disbelief and added, "Feel honored." He turned and walked away. Sara and several of her friends ran over asking me what he said. As they had watched the scene unfold, they became increasingly nervous, considering Nathan's reputation. When I told them, they were amazed. I realized then his public acknowledgment of me was the biggest compliment I could have ever received for helping to bring the town closer together.

My last day on the Yukon was much like the day I first arrived—hot, dusty, and the smell of moose skin hung in the air. I hugged Sara and told her I loved her. I promised her we'd be together again. Many of her friends doubted that, as many other Air Force men had made promises to other women in town only to change their minds once they got back home.

She said with tears in her eyes, "I believe you." I kissed her and jumped into the small two-seater Piper Cub and waved goodbye. The plane climbed over the tundra to the north and then turned around heading south circling Fort Yukon. I kept my eyes on Sara the entire time until I could see her no longer. As the plane crossed the Yukon River heading towards the mountains, I wiped the tears from my own eyes and looked forward to the future with anticipation.

Summer flew by and before I knew it, I was living in Minnesota, enrolled in a technical school in downtown Minneapolis—the plan, to become an electrician. I had absolutely no interest in such a vocation, but electricians made great money. However, without any real passion for this, my interest in the electrician vocation soon faded. Much to my mother's dismay, I completed one semester, then quit and joined a rock band called the Suspects. I also made friends with the guitarist, Chris, who was a great player and a cool guy. Together we found an apartment to help minimize expenses, and he had no problem with Sara moving in when she arrived from Alaska.

January raced in to Minneapolis with subzero temperatures and bitter winds that cut through a person like a knife. My days in Alaska had prepared me for surviving a Minnesota winter, and waiting for the bus every morning gave me a sense of accomplishment if I arrived at work without my fingers being so cold I couldn't move them for ten minutes. And if the bus ran late, as it always did on the coldest, snowiest days, my hands were so stiff by the time the bus arrived I could hardly toss quarters into the till.

When Sara finally arrived in Minneapolis, I didn't realize how much I had missed her and how much I really cared for her. Soon, Sara found a job working as a secretary for an electronics firm while I found a better paying job working the phones for a new alternative long-distance company called MCI. I managed to also audition for a band called Sky, since Suspects had by this time broken up. Sky had been together since high school and sang great harmonies. I worked hard for the audition but didn't make the cut, later learning I lost the gig because I had no car, and they did not want to pick me up every time we practiced.

One Friday night Sara and I went to a local bar, and after drinking a lot, I confessed I had been unfaithful to her during our time apart. I explained it was a one-night stand and that I never saw the woman again. At first she seemed to understand and wasn't as upset as I had expected. However, as the night wore on she began to drink more and more. By the end of the night she was yelling at me and hitting me and crying. I felt horrible. I had hurt the one person in my life I cared the most about.

I tried everything I could to make up for it, but it was impossible. I destroyed the most important part of a relationship—trust. She began to drink more often and became increasingly upset with me over just about anything—I knew there wasn't going to be a way to repair the damage I had caused.

On top of my hurting Sara in such a deep way, she felt overwhelmed by life in a large city. Adjusting to a strange and fast-paced culture proved to be a difficult and depressing dilemma for her. She felt alone, surrounded by a city of white people where few could relate to her. Fort Yukon wasn't just a small town. It was a town made up of a few main families that were all related to each other, a town of one large extended family. She never felt alone there. Now she was living in Minneapolis far from home, and the only person close to her had betrayed her. Ten months after Sara arrived in Minneapolis, she said goodbye and returned to Alaska.

A few weeks later, I received a call from Darrin, the lead singer of Sky, asking if I was still available, because if I was, they now wanted me. Quickly I accepted the offer, and later that night he dropped off the set list telling me I had ten days to learn forty songs. I felt intimidated by the guys in Sky because I knew they were each better musicians than I. They also sang great harmonies together, of which I had little experience. However, I managed to learn the material in time and made it through the first gig.

Surprisingly, the band used very little drugs. We had decided and could clearly see that, although we liked the highs, they were really more of a detriment than a help as far as our music was concerned. And because we took our music very seriously, the drugs had to go.

Although living the life of a band on the road had many seemingly great rewards, the only really satisfying part was performing on stage. The backstabbing managers, agents and psychotic bar owners made life difficult. I loved playing music, but the rest was hard to take.

The band continued gaining a good reputation and with it, larger crowds. For me, although I loved playing music, the real draw was being able to meet more women. It was amazing—we were just regular guys in a small local band, and yet so many women were attracted to us for that very reason. I took full advantage of that situation. One-night stands dominated my life and I seldom became serious with any woman. The women and the drinking kept the reality of a very empty life at bay. At times, when I would allow myself to think about it, I felt lonely and empty—lonely for that special someone in my life and an emptiness in my heart I just could not explain or understand. But the next wild party or band gig was beckoning me down the road, and at the time I saw no other path to take.

Altered States

Nirvana

"Well Brian, what did you think? Did you reach the nirvana of nothingness?" My new Transcendental Meditation teacher questioned me with a look of expectancy.

"Yes," I answered ecstatically. "I reached the nirvana all right... this is amazing!" Amazing didn't come close to describing this new experience. It was as if all thought from my mind just disappeared. Time seemed to stand still. No, this wasn't just amazing, it was out of this world!

Having tried just about everything else that crossed my path in order to find some peace of mind and satisfaction, when an upbeat sweet girl named Karen suggested I try meditation, I jumped at the chance. On top of being very health-conscious, Karen meditated twice a day without fail and convinced me to do the same. She said Transcendental Meditation (TM) kept her focused and calm. I was intrigued with this whole meditation concept but was only familiar with TM from the notoriety it received when the Beatles made it famous. Karen insisted meditation was a genuine way to relieve stress. Wanting to know about this, and definitely feeling the need for it, I asked Karen to sign me up for the Transcendental Meditation class.

The class took place once a week with sessions lasting four weeks. The cost was $400 per person, but for students it was $200. I lied and told them I was attending classes part-time. The teacher, Marta, accepted my check and began the class one-on-one. During the classes I learned about TM's history, its founder (the Maharishi Mahesh Yogi) and what to expect from it. She explained I would be given a mantra, a unique word I would say over and over again in my mind. She said the word had no meaning but was really just a sound.

When we were finally given our mantra during the third class session, Marta told me I could not share it with anyone. Sharing the mantra would reduce its power by making it common, she warned. She instructed me to say the word over and over out loud and then slowly make it softer until I was only saying it in my mind.

Marta explained that as I meditated, my mind would probably wander. "Let your thoughts appear and then slowly erase them by bringing back the mantra into your mind through repetition," she instructed. As I repeated the mantra, my thoughts would come and go, but I was able to make them disappear and then return to my mantra. While repeating the mantra over and over, I began to experience something I had never gone through before—I lost all thoughts, even though time was still passing and I was no longer repeating the mantra. Suddenly I realized I had reached and achieved the nothingness Marta had described. I had reached the goal of erasing all thoughts from my mind. No thoughts, then no mantra, and then nothing.

As I left the class that night, Karen was waiting outside for me. "Don't *you* look happy," she said.

"I am. What a powerful experience. That was far beyond anything I could've imagined."

"That time in between thoughts is where you reach the calmness," Karen explained. "The longer you practice, the longer you can hold time without thought. That is what they mean by achieving nirvana."

"I can't believe one word could have such power," I said in utter astonishment.

"It is not the word that holds any power Brian; it is the repetition and experiencing the silence," she responded.

Not sure what I was reaching out to in that nothingness, I felt satisfied and calm after the meditation, just like a baby resting peacefully in its mother's arms. As the weeks passed, not only did I feel this sense of peace and empowerment, I knew something else was going on, yet it seemed just beyond my comprehension. *Perhaps that is what Karen describes as a universal power that ties all things together.* Whatever it was, I was intrigued by it and wanted to know more. And yet, no matter how much I meditated this *something* seemed just beyond my reach. I could never quite grasp it. Having to meditate twice a day took quite a bit of discipline. Eventually, and largely due to Karen and me breaking up, I lost interest in TM.

Once again I poured myself into playing music with a local band. Still hoping I had what it took to become successful in music, I focused on writing music with the keyboard player from Sky. I was sure if I stuck it out long enough I could make it as a serious musician. I had just turned thirty and had become disillusioned with the whole dating scene, having gone from one woman to the next with no commitment or devotion on either side. I felt more ready than ever to pursue a lasting, serious relationship.

And so at a friend's wedding, when someone introduced me to one of the bridesmaids, I thought maybe things could be different this time. Hailey was wearing a sea-foam green dress and later joked that she'd never wear a dress like that except at a best friend's wedding. This pretty, vivacious girl had a sparkle to her personality, and I found her very charming. She was funny, witty, opinionated and completely uninhibited. We hit it off right away, and it wasn't too long before I fell head over heels for her.

Hailey reminded me of the female character, *Diane*, from the television series, "Cheers." She was very artsy and well-read, but unlike Diane never pretended to be so innocent. She had developed a raw edge from working within the theater community surrounded by union stagehands. She was a very talented set designer and builder and one of the few women that held such a position. Unfortunately, she suffered an injury just before she met me, forcing her to give up the job she loved so much. When we met, she had been trying to figure out what she wanted to do with her life. With the ending of a promising career, being forced to find another, and having a father who was dying of cancer, she too was facing a crossroads in her life. Meeting couldn't have come at a better time for both of us.

When it came to our beliefs, Hailey and I were in sync. She

too believed that many paths led to God, and to believe only one way existed was ridiculous. She also held the same disdain for Christians as I did. As far as she was concerned, Christians were small-minded, judgmental and unable to let go of all their restrictions that their religion had placed upon them. They had a rule against everything, especially sex.

Hailey introduced me to what I would now call the New Age, but at the time I saw it as an exciting way to reach God; the New Age was filled with intrigue and possibilities. I began to believe every person had within them innate untapped powers that could be accessed by letting go of the fears and the logical mindset of today's western Judeo-Christian culture. Although I wasn't a Christian, I found I still held many of those beliefs and values. Through my relationship with Hailey, I realized I needed to let go of those old-fashioned traditions, now believing that that controlling mindset held me back from all the things in life in which I hoped to aspire—love, success and wealth. Before meeting Hailey, I had somehow convinced myself I didn't deserve all these things. Through Hailey, I finally found freedom from all the bonds that held me down, no longer feeling like a prisoner tied to the railroad tracks of man-made boundaries.

Unlimited Power

I began studying the teachings of a man named Anthony Robbins, and he soon became my hero. Through these studies, I believed I could become successful and confident. In the early nineties, Anthony had become the guru of positive thinking and success. He wrote *Unlimited Power* and had a series of tapes called *Personal Power*, which taught a new way of thinking. The basis for his theory was called Neurolinguistic Programming or NLP for short. His explanation of NLP made perfect sense to me:

> [T]he name comes from "neuro," referring to the brain, and "linguistic," referring to language. Programming is the installation of a plan or procedure. NLP is the study of how language, both verbal and nonverbal, affects our

nervous system. Our ability to do anything in life is based upon our ability to direct our own nervous system. Those who are able to produce some outstanding result do so by producing specific communications to and through the nervous system.[1]

One of the methods Robbins used was called "anchoring." Imagine being able to bring yourself back to a time when you felt great and could immediately access those emotions at anytime you wanted. He explained:

[Y]ou can create a consistent triggering mechanism that will automatically cause you to create the state that you desire in any situation without your having to think about it.[2]

I understood his description by having to think back to a time in my life of great success:

Really think about it and let yourself feel it. Then pick a part of your body like the tip of your right pinky and squeeze it during this great memory. Now every time you want to feel good and confident, simply squeeze that finger and all the emotions come flooding back.

I followed all his methods to see if I could change my destiny. If I could erase all my old thoughts of feeling like a loser, I could move on and succeed. Much to my dismay however, while I followed his methods to a tee, my life remained pretty much the same and I continued living a meager existence without peace or direction.

I discovered a book called *The Celestine Prophesy* written by James Redfield, and it became a favorite of mine. Every one I knew seemed to be reading and discussing The *Celestine Prophesy*. The description on the cover of the book reads:

In the rain forests of Peru, an ancient manuscript has been discovered. Within its pages are nine key insights

into life itself—insights each human being is predicted to
grasp sequentially, one insight then another, as we move
toward a completely spiritual culture on Earth.[3]

The Celestine Prophecy contained mysteries that are supposedly
changing our world. Drawing on ancient wisdom, it explains how to
make connections among the events happening right now ... and
lets the reader see what is going to happen in the years to come![4]
The book was, of course, a fictional story, but the insights themselves caught on. The first insight described the notion that there
are no "chance" coincidences. In other words, every event in a
person's life must be viewed through the prism that it was meant to
have happened. By paying attention to seemingly "Chance Coincidences" and by following them, these "synchronistic events" develop paths of "spiritual truth."[5] Not only that, but the book taught
how easy it is to read people and know who they are and what they
are feeling because of an energy that surrounds each person.
As understanding is gained, a connection with the energy that
makes up the universe itself can be obtained. It is the ultimate state of
consciousness to believe we are all a part of this earth and each other
and can become beings of light, connecting with God's energy. The
answer to life's questions would be over. Sin does not exist, neither
does right or wrong, just each person following his own intuition
through meditation, dreams and those mysterious coincidences. This
eventually leads to the ultimate transformation, as Redfield describes
in the Ninth Insight which he calls *The Emerging Culture*:

> As we all evolve toward the best completion of our
> spiritual missions, the technological means of survival
> will be fully automated as humans focus instead on
> synchronistic growth. Such growth will move humans
> into higher energy states, ultimately transforming our
> bodies into spiritual form and uniting this dimension
> of existence with the after-life dimension, ending the
> cycle of birth and death.[6]

If I could just tap into this energy and understand it, perhaps then I could change my life, bring about my destiny and achieve all I wanted. I now believed I had the power within, but how to bring it out of myself remained a mystery. I was sure a world of untapped energy surrounded me and every other human being, just waiting for each of us to take hold of it—finally within reach. Redfield's philosophy became the cornerstone of my entire existence. I had no doubt about its power and the possibility of it working.

Someone to Love

I was living with my friend Steve at the time, a drummer in my new band. He was a very spiritual person, and we shared the same view about life. He, Hailey and I got along great as we shared the same views about God. We often talked about the concept of a God of love that simply accepted a human being as he or she was and certainly had no plans of punishment or Hell, like the Christian concept of God. And since sin or evil did not exist, there sure wasn't a need for a Savior dying on a *cross*.

Hailey and I grew closer as the months passed, and we began talking of a future together. Steve began to see the writing on the wall and knew Hailey and I would eventually move in together. I told Hailey that because of my past experiences, I was not willing to live with a woman again without a clear commitment to marriage sometime in the future.

Although Hailey's mom didn't approve of us living together, she knew I cared deeply about Hailey and was very serious with my intentions towards her daughter. We found a place in the northern suburbs and started setting up house. I decided—well perhaps Hailey decided—that my bachelor-style furniture would have to go; I watched in wonder as Hailey transformed the place into an intrinsically-designed work of art.

At the time Hailey and I moved in together, I was a sales representative for an art wholesaler. I virtually went door to door to every business in town selling art for their offices. I was on commission only and learned quite a bit about reading people and how to get them to buy. It was a great education in people skills and sales, and Hailey was always impressed with my ability to start off with zero on Monday and have enough to pay the bills by Friday.

During this time Hailey started her own business selling fitness products. I was too busy with my art business to participate fully, but I supported her when I could.

We shared one weakness—we were both unrealistic about money and how to plan for a solid financial future. We lived with the premise that within six months both of our businesses would succeed, and we would be rich. That mistake haunted us for years to come.

We had a beautiful garden wedding among close friends, and our new pastor from Unity Church married us. I was sure that being married and committed to one woman would help bring fulfillment and satisfaction to my life as well as Hailey's.

We had started attending Unity on the recommendation of one of Hailey's friends. I had never attended a church like this and was often confused about their beliefs. Their description of Jesus was much different than the Jesus I had heard about as a child. *Their* Jesus was referred to in a metaphysical way—a perfect example of what man could become by opening the mind to the realization we were all God or God-like. Jesus became the Christ because he knew it was possible. They referred to him as one of the great masters, like Buddha. He was put on this Earth to teach us lessons. Contrasting my childhood Jesus, I liked this new version far better. The Christian version was one of rules and consequences, and if you didn't follow him only, you were destined to Hell.

Unity's philosophy taught that there were no *right* answers, and we should accept all people's ideas about God. Each person was on his or her own journey to finding truth. Our pastor once said, "You could go over the mountain, around the mountain or underneath the mountain, but there is no wrong way to reach God. We all end up in the same place."

One night while Hailey and I were at home, I received a phone call. I was surprised to hear Sara's voice on the other end. She said she was sorry for everything that had happened between us and regretted her behavior. I assured her I held no animosity towards her. She then told me she had gone to Alcoholics Anonymous and admitted she was an alcoholic. She said she had made many mistakes while we were together and wanted to apologize. I told her I had made many mistakes also and that apologies were not necessary after so long a period had passed.

"How did you find the strength to overcome your addiction, Sara," I asked with sincere interest.

"I found Jesus Christ, Brian, and he has given me the strength." She said the Lord had healed her, and she no longer had any fears. She then inquired about my own spiritual state. I told her my wife and I were attending Unity Church. She was happy to hear I had gotten married, but I could tell she was uncomfortable with my choice of churches. She asked what they believed about Jesus, and I said he is one of the great teachers from whom we can all learn. She seemed anxious about this and tried to explain that Jesus was the only way.

At this point Hailey, who was listening to this conversation, told me to hang up. I told Sara I was very satisfied with my spirituality and I didn't need to be *saved* as she put it. She then told me Unity Church was wrong and Jesus wasn't a great master or a great teacher, but he was God.

"You can believe that if you wish Sara, but don't try pushing your religion down my throat." She tried arguing the point with me, but I felt confident I had advanced far beyond her level of thinking. I abruptly said goodbye and hung up.

After I shared with Hailey what Sara had said, she scoffed, "What is it about these *born-again* types? They are so narrow-minded. It is *their* way or nothing. Why do they think we need saving?"

I laughed and said with an exaggerated preacher voice, "Because you are all sinners, and you're going to Hell unless you accept Jeeeee-sus."

Hailey laughed and said, "Well, I guess we are going to Hell then."

"At least we will be together," I responded. We both had a good laugh about that.

A few months after our wedding, the growth from our businesses was significantly less than we had expected. However, I believed if I kept a positive attitude, we would soon be fine. Based upon that belief, we bought a house we could not afford.

One day, Hailey met a woman teaching a course called *Magnetizing and Manifesting*. The course was designed to release full financial potential by addressing the spiritual blocks that caused hindrance. Hailey knew that although I could go out everyday and sell art, I still suffered from great self-doubt and a limited belief system about wealth and prosperity.

Carolyn, a tall attractive woman with long dark hair taught the course. She was not at all what I expected. She had a great business sense and was not ashamed about building or accepting financial progress. Most of the spiritual people I had met in the past seemed to shun money or believe that wealth accumulation was evil. She did not believe that at all.

Carolyn believed that all had the potential but few really believed it themselves. The class, made up of six women and myself, was a series of guided meditations and a discussion of what each of us experienced during these meditations. Carolyn would run a rubber mallet inside a large crystal bowl, making a long steady tone that lasted for a minute or more.

Carolyn then instructed us to lie on the floor, close our eyes and imagine we were lying in a field of wildflowers on a beautiful summer's day. The wind was calm, and the smell of flowers awakened our senses. As we were lying in the field, she asked us to now leave our bodies and look down upon ourselves. Carolyn then guided us to raise our souls to the heavens and to leave our earthly bodies behind. When we reached what we believed to be the outer edges of the universe she told us to ask for a message from the universe and what we needed to know at this time. "Listen to the voice inside you. Ask what it is you need to know to help you release the burdens you carry," she said softly.

The room grew very silent, and then a voice inside me said, "Brian you are not a bad person. Nothing you do is wrong in my eyes. You are too hard on yourself. You are loved and are released from all guilt. Listen to me and allow me to guide you. I will never lead you astray."

Carolyn's voice began softly saying, "Let us return back to Earth and to that warm fragrant field." The meditation ended, and we all shared our thoughts and feelings. I left the session with a sense that a kind and loving power had been waiting for me all my life, and now I had access to it.

My business with the art company was doing quite well, and I had built a solid clientele. I had many repeat customers and one of them, Jake, owned a large construction company. He often called, asking me to bring over any new art that came in. One day after making a call to his office he invited me to lunch. During lunch we talked about a wide range of topics as we often did. I shared with him the classes I was taking, but this seemed to really distress him. "I am a Christian, Brian," he began. "Because of what I believe, I wouldn't be able to get involved in something like that."

I was shocked to find out he was a Christian. He had seemed so normal, and I also knew from previous conversations he was very wealthy. "I thought Christians frowned upon success and wealth," I said to him, as I pondered his confession of being one of those Christians.

He looked surprised, "Who told you that?"

"Doesn't the Bible say money is the root of all evil?" I asked, very curious as to how he would answer.

"No, it doesn't say that," he replied. He reached into his desk and pulled out a large Bible. Within a few seconds he found the quote and began reading out loud, "'For the *love* of money is a root of all kinds of evil.' That's from I Timothy 6:10. God doesn't say that money is evil." Jake continued, "But He does say man can get caught up in his riches so much he forgets where his prosperity comes from and becomes miserly and greedy." He leaned across his desk and said, "Brian, everything I have is because of God. He is the source, not me. God knows people need my skills to build their homes and buildings. He also knows many men need jobs to feed their families, and I do my best to make sure they are working." He continued, "Money can make a man powerful and so content he thinks he doesn't need God. He is wrong." He laughed and said, "Guess what? How much do riches matter after you are dead? I seek God first in my life. Everything else comes second."

"What if God took away your business and all your money?" I asked.

"Then I would see that God must have a different plan for me, and I would accept it." His answer surprised me. He continued, "However, I really don't worry about that. The Bible tells me not to worry because God promises to take care of me and my family. He opened the Bible again and read:

> And which of you by worrying can add one cubit to his stature? If you then are not able to do the least, why are you anxious for the rest? Consider the lilies, how they grow: they neither toil nor spin; and yet I say to you, even Solomon in all his glory was not arrayed like one of these. If then God so clothes the grass, which today is in the field and tomorrow is thrown into the oven, how much more will He clothe you, O you of little faith?

> And do not seek what you should eat or what you should drink, nor have an anxious mind. For all these things the nations of the world seek after, and your Father knows that you need these things. But seek the kingdom of God, and all these things shall be added to you. (Luke 12: 25-31)

Suddenly a frown found itself on his usually smiling face, "Brian, you are messing with powers that are not good. Be careful with these classes you are taking."

Sitting back in my chair, trying to look as relaxed and at ease as possible, I answered, "Everything I'm getting out of it seems good to me."

Sounding unconvinced he said, "Hmmm, it always starts that way."

I didn't challenge him further as he was one of my best clients. I thought if we got into a real argument over religion he might not call me anymore. As I drove away from his office his words about God, money and evil played over and over in my mind like a broken record. It all seemed rather confusing to me. God was his source, but why wasn't my version of God okay? What difference did it make whether I meditated to the power of the universe to gain my prosperity or the God of the Bible? Aren't they all just the same source with different names? Like the firm foundations of a steel-girded building, my beliefs in how I viewed God were not about to be shaken at the words of a *Bible-thumping* Christian. I had spent far too many years developing and grooming my arguments and reasoning in spiritual matters to cave in now.

Hailey and I had been married two years and were living in a beautiful town home, which we struggled to pay for each month, even though both of us were working several part-time jobs. When I left the Air Force, the one aspect I gleaned from the experience was how to pay bills and be responsible when it came to money. But during the years with Hailey, I forgot every lesson I had been taught. Instead of seeking one good-paying job, I worked part-time at several so I could assist Hailey with her fitness-product business. The money never came in from that business, and before we knew it we were in a financial downward spiral.

Universal Energy

Hailey and I began fighting over money all the time, and our relationship began to show signs of strain and wear. My self-confidence was taking a beating. I was depressed, and I had completely lost any spirituality I previously had. I found it difficult to maintain a connection with the unifying universal energy while fighting with my wife and struggling to stay financially afloat.

Hailey and Steve started taking a year long course that promised to teach how to perform psychic readings. As the months slipped by, they would often describe to me what they were learning, and did it ever sound intriguing. I had no real interest in performing psychic readings, but the connection they were building with God or the universe was what I wanted desperately. Half way through their course, I decided I too wanted to join such a class.

Elinor Moon, the woman who would teach my class had long flowing blond hair and eyes that looked like blue moons, fitting her name perfectly. Sitting on the couch that first session, I couldn't help but wonder whether this would even work. Hailey gave me the heads up that at the first meeting the instructor would perform a reading on me. I was skeptical and determined to test this woman. I wasn't going to fall for anything phony. Many times on television I had seen psychics ask leading questions of their subject trying to glean information from them and then act like they knew all along. My strategy was to stay as silent as possible and when she asked questions, I would be very vague with my answers.

She started by asking me a few general questions about how I heard about her and why I was taking the class. I told her about my wife's experience and that I was very intrigued by the sense of peace she experienced and the feeling of connection with the universe she had gained.

Elinor Moon smiled and said, "Okay, let's begin." She closed her eyes for a few moments and then began to share with me what she was *seeing*. She told me she saw a strained relationship with my father and growing tension in my marriage. She was certainly right about both those points, but maybe she was just guessing. She had a puzzled look on her face and said, "You think a lot don't you?"

"What do you mean?"

She paused and said, "You calculate things constantly. You think about every aspect of things and you count numbers in your head when you are tense or frustrated." She continued, "When things were tense at home when you were young, this is how you would escape." She paused, then asked, "Am I correct? You would escape into your mind, right?"

My mouth dropped open, and I could feel my muscles tightening. She couldn't have been more right. All of my life, I had been a constant thinker, trying to figure things out, always evaluating distances, what is being said, what things mean. Whenever I became impatient, I counted numbers in my head to get a grip on myself.

"Yes," I said with a sense of awe—I had never once told anyone this. "Hmmm," she said. "Very interesting. I have never met anyone like you before." At the end of the session she said, "Here is the message I want you to hear Brian. You are not a failure. That's what I'm being told to tell you." The words hit me hard as my eyes became moist—the very core of my being had been touched, and emotion welled up within me. "Brian, I think I can help you, and I definitely think this class will help you. Are you still interested?"

"Yes, I am," I replied. I was still reeling from the information she shared.

She smiled and said, "The cost of the class is $20 each week, and it will last one year." The cost for today's reading is $80. I thanked her and gave her the money. She walked me to the door and said, "See you Wednesday night."

I thanked her and drove home with a feeling of encouragement and a sense of awe of what I had just experienced. How could she have known those things? I wasn't sure how, but I wanted to know more.

One of Hailey's business associates was a woman named June. We had gotten to know both her and her husband, Alan, through the business. They were a very friendly and kind couple, and we enjoyed their company. Hailey shared with me that June and Alan were born-again Christians. We both were a little uncomfortable with that, but it didn't stop us from becoming friends with them. Hailey and I would joke about the shock they would have if they knew what we were involved in and for sure condemn us to Hell. However, when Hailey did eventually share with them her philosophy about God, she said they said very little and didn't act judgmental in any way. I could tell they were concerned about us but never portrayed an attitude of condemnation. Perhaps that is why we didn't feel threatened by them but rather were drawn to them because of their kindness, their calm demeanor and perhaps the need we had for an older and wiser couple in our lives.

Through all the challenges Hailey and I were facing in our marriage and in our financial difficulties, it was nice to know we had two understanding people to talk to. Occasionally, June invited us to their church, but neither of us had any interest. I was much more interested in starting the class than facing a building filled with a bunch of *Jesus freaks*.

Soon the night came for my first class. I arrived at Elinor's place a little early to begin the class, which consisted of three women and me. When we were all seated, we went around the room, introducing ourselves and sharing why we decided to take the class. Ann was a friend of Hailey's that she had met at Unity Church. Hailey was now teaching Sunday school, and Ann's two teenage daughters were in her class. Ann shared how she had become overwhelmed with raising two daughters on her own and needed some guidance in her life.

Alison, one of the other girls, was in her late twenties and said she was struggling to find her identity. She had recently shared with her parents that she was lesbian, and although they affirmed their love for her, they were confused and concerned about what this meant for her life. Elinor shared that she too was lesbian and hoped this class would help Alison find the assurance she was looking for.

I shared with the group how I struggled with my self-confidence and was looking for meaning in my life. Feeling a freedom to be open and honest, I described my fear of losing everything important to me if I didn't come to grips with my problems and find some solid solutions. I shared with them that my wife was taking the same class, and I hoped this would bring us closer together and give us a greater understanding of each other.

The last to speak was May. She was in her early fifties and shared that she had been divorced for many years. She had resigned herself to the reality that she was too old to get remarried and wanted to know how to better cope with the reality that she was going to be alone for the rest of her life. Elinor smiled and said, "I can assure you that by the end of these classes none of you will ever feel alone again."

The class began with a meditation exercise that we were to practice everyday when we awoke and again each evening. Elinor instructed us to sit with our feet firmly on the ground and to close our eyes. She then asked us to imagine roots or cords extending from the soles of our feet down into the earth. She said to imagine going deeper and deeper to the light, with the heat and power of the earth below us. Her words flowed from one to another and had an almost hypnotic effect on me:

> Once the cords reach a certain point, attach the cords to that power. Bring that energy up those roots, up through the soles of your feet, up your legs, and allow them to attach to the base of your spine to the first Chakra. You are now grounded in earth's energy.

I finally felt I was heading in the right direction and tapping into a world and an energy that would give guidance and insight.

Each week in class we were given a new practice to follow and before too long, I began to notice a presence or strength come over me. I seemed to be more keenly aware of myself and what others were thinking even when they didn't say anything. *I am able to read the thoughts of other people and know what they are thinking. This is far more empowering than I had expected.* I believed I really was reading the minds of those around me.

Although Hailey and I both seemed to be gaining so much from our classes, our relationship continued to deteriorate. An intensity and cruelty now permeated all of our arguments. Our fighting escalated the boundaries of disagreements about money, the house or the usual arguments every couple has. It was personal and at times vicious. We knew each other's vulnerabilities, and we pushed those buttons in order to win an argument. Although we were never physically violent, never striking each other, our words were as hurtful as if we had been. I was quick to anger and exploded at Hailey for the slightest irritation or infraction.

With so much turmoil at home, going to class was a bright spot in my life. I never tired of this new source of knowledge, strength and energy. We learned the dynamics of meditation and added more and more exercises to use during each of our meditations. The grounding portion was only the beginning of ten steps to take before we were ready to perform readings. We called it *running our energy*.

The next step in the process of performing readings and in meditating was to gather energy from the universe. As we finished our grounding exercise, Elinor asked us to keep our eyes closed and imagine a funnel appearing above our heads. She said, "Imagine all of the psychic energy from the heavens pouring down through that funnel, through your seventh chakra on the crown of your head. Then allow that energy to follow down your spine and connect with earth's energy in your first chakra at the base of your spine." She continued, "You are now connected to earth's energy and the psychic energy of the universe."

"Next," she said, "run that energy up and down your spine from the first chakra up to the base of your skull and then back down again. Keep that energy going up and down, up and down," she repeated. "Now direct that energy to move in a figure eight, circling the first chakra and then going up to your head, circling it and back down again, over and over and over again," she said softly. We stayed in that state for several minutes. After a while, she told us to open our eyes and instructed each one of us to describe our experience and our feelings.

"I feel so powerful, so connected to something," May began. "It's like energy coursing through my body."

"Like electricity," Alison added. We all nodded in agreement.

"How about you Brian?" Elinor asked.

"I feel more alive than I ever have before—like tapping into the very source of all power and knowledge. Nothing scary or uncomfortable about this. I feel like I've just been showered by a loving energy." The others agreed. Delighted that we had been so successful, Elinor spoke to us as if we were her children and had just won a championship baseball game with a shutout score. "That's wonderful," she said. "Let's take a break."

During the break, Ann shared with me how her children were learning some of the same exercises from Hailey at Sunday school. She was teaching them the grounding technique. Ann elaborated, "I noticed one morning both my girls were meditating. I was so proud of both of them." Ann boasted, "They say it helps them focus at school better. By the way, they adore Hailey. She really connects with young people like no one I have ever seen before."

"She loves kids and loves to be around them," I said. Ann was right. Hailey was happiest when she was surrounded by a group of kids.

Chakras

In June we began to examine the chakras and their alleged meanings. The word chakra is Sanskrit for wheel or disk and is said to signify one of seven basic energy centers in the body. Each of these centers supposedly correlates to major nerve ganglia branching forth from the spinal column. The chakras are also supposed to be related to levels of consciousness, developmental stages of life, colors, sounds, body functions and so on.

The following list describes each chakra and gives a New Age explanation of their supposed spiritual, emotional, and physical make-up:

> First chakra (Root): Located at base of the spine, connected to survival instincts, and to a sense of trust and grounding; brings sense of health, prosperity, security, and dynamic presence.

> The second chakra (Orange): Located in the abdomen, lower back, and sexual organs, is related to the element water, and to emotions and sexuality; provides sense of connection to others through feeling, desire, sensation, and movement.

> The third chakra (Solar Plexus): Known as the power chakra; gives us a sense of freedom, power, control and ease of being; brings energy, effectiveness, spontaneity, and non-dominating power.

> The fourth chakra (Heart): Related to perceptions of love and opposites in the psyche: mind and body, male and female, persona and shadow, ego and unity; gives

an ability to love, feel compassion, and have a deep sense of peace and centeredness.

The fifth chakra (Throat): Located in the throat and is related to our expressing communication and creativity and also receiving.

The sixth chakra (Brow): Related to the act of seeing, both physically and spiritually; this is the place where true motivations are found.

The seventh chakra (Crown): Relates to consciousness and gives a sense of empathy towards others; brings knowledge, wisdom, understanding, spiritual connection, and bliss.

Elinor showed us how to meditate and focus on each of the seven chakras. We were able to read how each of these energy vortexes related to our lives, the blockages to awareness, and our emotions.

She shared with us how blockages in these energy centers may be the root cause of the blocks in our lives. As each week progressed we concentrated on each chakra in an attempt to identify the blocks. Elinor said the removal of these blocks may take a long time but for now to just be aware of them.

In July, I decided to take a business trip to California. It was a large meeting of people sharing ideas and experiences to make their businesses grow. Our friends, June and Alan, happened to be going also.

Hailey decided not to go with me to the meeting as she was now quite busy teaching classes in our home to kids from Sunday school. She had become quite a hit with all the parents as she had been performing readings on them, and they gave her much praise and attention for these successes. It was becoming a very fulfilling lifestyle for both of us.

On my business trip, I spent several days going to classes on entrepreneurship, maintaining the proper business attitude, and the future of the market place. Knowing virtually no one except for

June and Alan, I spent most of my time with them. Every so often, June questioned me about the classes Hailey and I had been taking. Though she didn't say much, I could tell through her facial expressions she did not approve of our doing the classes. Often these conversations gave me the openings I needed to challenge her Christianity. Having now become a master at going after the Achilles heel of Christians, especially the born-again ones, I made it clear to June I would not and could not ever accept her way of believing.

Over dinner one evening, I asked, "If God is a loving and forgiving God, why do you say some people will go to Hell? Shouldn't everyone go to Heaven?"

June replied, "God doesn't want people to go to Hell—that is why He sent Jesus to the Earth."

"I don't understand this," I argued. "He is supposedly a loving God, but He turns his back on everyone who isn't a Christian?"

A friend of June's, Elaine, sat quietly listening to the conversation then finally said, "People don't go to Hell because they aren't Christians; they go to Hell because they have no way of absolving themselves of sin."

She continued, "Brian, let me give you an analogy. In a sense, God is allergic to sin. He loves you, but He can't be around sin."

Frustrated and offended at her insinuation that I was a bad person, I snapped, "But I am not a sinner. I am a good person."

She replied calmly, "But you are not perfect, and you can make mistakes in your life. That is sin, and we are all in sin because of the original sin."

"Original sin? What is *that*," I asked, beginning to feel exasperated.

"When Adam and Eve defied God," Elaine continued, "sin began, and we have been paying for that mistake ever since."

I replied defiantly, "You really believe that story? That is a mythical story. No one really believes that."

"I do, completely," she replied. June and Alan both said they believed it also.

I said, "Okay, that's your belief system, and I respect that, but what is wrong with mine? My way is as right as yours. God loves me, and He will accept me as I am. I do not need to join your religion for God to love me. Religion was created by man, not by God anyway." I then asked, "Do you really believe God only likes Christians, and to Hell with the Hindus?"

June replied, "God doesn't dislike anyone, but He wants us to know the truth about Him. His Son existed with God and as God from all eternity (John 1:1), and then the Father sent the Son. It is not God's fault many have rejected His message."

"So I am going to Hell then?" I said impetuously.

June and Alan said with sincerity, "If you are open to listening to His message, God will reveal His truth to you."

I felt very defensive, and I knew they were frustrated with my questions. "I'm sorry. I just can't accept your version of God," I replied.

Elaine said, "It isn't our version of God if the story of Jesus is true. We didn't make up this story Brian."

She then asked, "Brian if the story of Jesus is true, then we know who God is, and the mystery is over, isn't it?"

I was confused by the question, "I'm not sure. What do you mean?"

She asked, "If God reveals Himself and says, 'Here I am, this is the truth about me,' then doesn't it make sense that all other theories about God would be irrelevant?"

I pondered the question and said, "But the problem is we do not know that the story is true. Because it came out of a book 2000 years old, and it has been translated and mistranslated so many times, no one knows what it originally said." My stomach was churning now. Nothing they said made any sense. I felt like I was about to break down and cry, and I didn't understand why.

After dinner we made our way back to the hotel. June came up behind me and put her hand on my shoulder and said, "Brian, I hope you know we were not trying to hurt your feelings. We really care about you and Hailey. We are concerned about you, that's all. We are worried about you."

I knew she was telling the truth and that she really did care. "I know, but I'm doing fine. June, I just can't accept what you are telling me." The last thing I wanted was to become a Christian. The very idea made me feel ill. I had a class that was answering all my questions, and I really didn't feel the need to change my life, especially not in *that* direction!

The next morning I went to the lobby to catch the bus to the convention center. As I boarded one of the buses that was waiting to transport us, one quick glance and I could see only two seats available. I grabbed the seat next to a guy who appeared to be my age. "Morning," I said.

Followed by a big yawn, he nodded and mumbled, "Good morning."

"Stay up too late?" I queried, not really too interested but wanting to be polite.

"Yeah a little bit," he laughed. "I met with some friends last night I haven't seen in years. I used to play in a band out here in L.A.."

"Really? I played in a band for many years myself," I said.

"That's cool. My name is Kevin," he replied. While introducing myself, I shook his hand. For most of the bus trip we shared our many band-on-the-road stories.

When the bus pulled up to the convention center, we continued talking as we got off the bus and headed towards the entrance. "What do you do now?" I asked Kevin, genuinely interested in this friendly fellow who too had a love for music.

He replied, "I'm going to school to become a pastor."

I laughed and said, "Wow, what a change from musician to pastor."

He smiled and said, "Yeah, well life changes, and I felt the call to serve the Lord."

As we walked inside the hall he turned to me and asked, "Are you a Christian Brian?"

I replied with a bit of a laugh and said, "I consider myself a Catholic agnostic."

He looked puzzled. "What does *that* mean," he asked? Much like with those who had gone before, I gave him my usual smart-aleck and very well-rehearsed answer of being a Catholic agnostic who believes every religion and path to God is right.

He was about to speak when an attractive woman came up from behind him and gave him a hug. He turned to her and said, "Hi sweetie," and gave her a kiss. He turned back to me and said, "This is my wife, Carrie. Carrie, this is Brian,"

I reached out and shook her hand. We spoke briefly about the weather and the convention, then Carrie pulled on Kevin's hand and said, "We need to find our seats before we lose them." He agreed and turned back to me, "Brian you may want to rethink your theory on religion. There's only one truth, not many. Let's continue this conversation later, okay?"

Carrie pulled him into the crowd, and he was gone. I actually hoped we would be able to finish our talk as I had become curious about his beliefs and felt a certain draw to this stranger. But we would never finish that conversation as he had suggested for that was the last time I ever saw him—"Oh well," I thought later, shrugging my shoulders. "Just another long line of people I've run into during my life who have tried to convert me. But it will never work; I will never become one of them." And yet I felt a certain tug at my heart that night; something about that man hit a nerve deep within me. I couldn't describe it or understand it, but several months would pass before I could stop thinking about that encounter.

Guides From Another World

A sense of excitement and intrigue filled the air. Elinor just informed the class we were now ready to embark on the next stage of our training. "Have you ever asked yourself how it is possible to perform psychic readings without having any psychic ability of your own?" Elinor questioned the class. We all looked at each other and nodded. "The answer is you do not need any." She continued, "For the last six months you have been preparing yourselves for *assistants* to help you in performing these readings. Starting tonight we will begin to identify and later come to know your *spirit guides*—the ones who will assist you in your readings."

Elinor continued with this surprising and compelling instruction, "With your eyes closed, imagine an open doorway standing in front of you. Just focus on the frame of the door. Now, silently within your mind, ask the first guide to step in front of the door and reveal him or herself." She added, "It actually may not be male or female. Do not concern yourself with what they look like or how they appear." At first, as I stared at the doorway, I saw only blackness. Then, a moment later, a large figure appeared looking similar to a Viking or medieval soldier. He looked tough, strong and somewhat intimidating. Elinor went on, "Allow each one to appear before the door so that you become familiar with them."

The next to appear was a very meek looking woman with a warm smile. After her there came a smoke-like vapor rising from the floor. It swirled for a moment and then moved away. Next came a man of my age dressed casually. He smiled and spoke to me saying, "You and I are going to be close." He waved and stepped to the right to allow the next one to appear. This one was a solemn looking old man, tall and gaunt. He didn't smile or even seem to acknowledge me. He appeared and then faded back into darkness.

Elinor interrupted and told us to end our meditation. Before leaving, she instructed us to spend time during the week getting to know each guide. A hand shot up in class and the question was asked, "Why are there so many of them?"

To this, Elinor answered, "Because you may need different guides for different people on whom you perform readings. And you should know—these guides have always been there. This is just the first time you are seeing them, but they have always been there for you—protecting you and guiding you. Now that you know them, you can grow closer and learn from them." We were then dismissed. As I walked away, I felt a sense of awe and respect for these new *acquaintances*.

I shared my experience with Hailey and Steve only to learn they each had over fifteen guides they communicated with!

"Each person is surrounded by many spirit guides of his or her own," Steve began. "During a reading, our guides speak to that person's guides, and that communication is transferred to you. Sometimes the message is heard like a voice in your head, or it might be a picture telling you what you need to know."

Hailey likened the experience to going through someone's scrapbook and looking at all the things they have gathered and saved.

Steve told me he was doing a reading for a woman when he saw a doctor's medical bag. The woman gasped and said her dad was a doctor and that she kept his bag after his death. She said that during the move to her new home the bag was lost. She had such regret because it was her primary connection to her father and now she felt like she had let her father down.

Steve communicated to her that the guides told him her dad was not upset. The bag wasn't important, and the connection between herself and her father still existed. "Your dad is alive," Steve continued. "He still loves you and is proud of you." This immediately brought tears to the woman's eyes—soon she was crying softly. The reading had allowed her to forgive herself for the loss of the bag and for the regret she had over their relationship. "There's a great reward in performing a reading, knowing someone is really being helped. Why people think this is evil is beyond me. This is not evil," Steve assured me.

As the weeks passed, my meditation time increased and I spent more and more time getting to know the personalities of my spirit guides. The female figure, who always appeared translucent, became my most frequent guide during readings. She was very gentle and sweet and was the most encouraging to me when I felt discouraged. Another that I often used was the one who dressed casually in sweaters and khaki pants. It seemed odd that this was one of my spirit guides. He had a very strong assertive personality. He always encouraged me to take chances. He told me I was eventually going to be wealthy if I just trusted the universe to bring it to me.

I questioned Elinor about the appearance of my guides. She said they may appear to look in such a way that you can comprehend and trust. "Don't worry about it," she insisted. Elinor constantly reminded me I was trying too hard. She said I was thinking too much. "Stop analyzing it all, and just trust your feelings. The more you let go, the more you will be open to the spirit guides' abilities to teach you what you need to know."

Although Hailey and I were suffering financially, I decided to trust and let go and not worry whether we had enough money or not. The money would come if I just trusted. As the summer came to a close, we had progressed in our ability to run our energy and to converse with and contact our spirit guides. Each class member expressed how great this new empowering felt. Elinor informed us we were now ready to start readings on one another. Ann performed a reading for me and said the fall would hold great change for me, insisting the financial burden would be lifted from Hailey and me.

Elinor shared with us why she had us spend so much time getting to know our spirit guides. She asked, "Ann, you know Brian quite well by now don't you?"

"Yes, we have become friends through this class."

"Do you think that your knowledge of him might influence

your reading?" Elinor asked.

Ann paused for a moment and said, "Well, I suppose it might but ..."

Elinor continued, "I need to share with you some ethics that must be adhered to if you are to perform a responsible reading."

We all listened intently as Elinor continued:

> We all have prejudices or preconceived ideas about people. Those feelings can interfere with your reading. To make sure your ideas and influences do not distort the reading you must let go and allow your guides to speak through you. You are a vessel. Allow the guide to be unencumbered by your will. It is your will that will cause the reading to be wrong or inaccurate. You have been running your energy consistently for the past seven months and the door to the spirits' power has been opened. As the years go on, your readings will be better because you will allow yourself more and more to be a conduit.

Alison asked, "What if the person I am doing a reading for asks something like, 'Is my girlfriend going to leave me,' and I see the answer is yes, should I tell him?"

Elinor responded, "When someone asks a serious question and you know the answer is bad, look above his or her head and imagine a rose appearing above the head. If the rose is standing upright, you can speak the truth boldly. If it is upside down, do not."

"What would I say in such a situation?" Alison asked.

"Just say there doesn't seem to be a clear answer about this right now and then simply apologize."

From then on, I began performing readings for my friends at work, often amazing them with my accuracy in pinpointing unique circumstances. While I certainly did not get everything right, I believed I was able to give great insight into the lives of my fellow workers, helping them prepare for changes in their lives.

One day I did a reading for Rachel, one of the new women in

our department. She was very skeptical about allowing me to perform the reading but said she desperately needed to know something. She didn't say what it was, but I knew immediately to what she was referring. My translucent female guide whispered in my head, *"Tell her the answer is yes. She wants to know if she should stay with her boyfriend."* At the time I wasn't sure if I should be so bold to say this so I asked, "Rachel, does this have to do with your boyfriend?"

Rachel looked surprised and said "Yes!"

An image came into my head of a very pretty diamond ring. The voice whispered, *"Brian, what does that image tell you?"* I smiled and said, "Rachel, the answer is yes. You should stay with your boyfriend—he wants to marry you!"

Rachel's mouth dropped open. Her eyes filled with tears. "Oh my goodness," she cried. "Are you sure?"

Brian, wait! Something else is at work here. She has already started a relationship with someone else. She is tired of waiting for her boyfriend to make a commitment. Tell her that the other relationship should not go forward. I looked above her head and saw the rose standing up. Feeling the confirmation I needed to proceed, I said, "The answer to your other question is, end it. Do not stray from your boyfriend. He wants you, but you need to remain patient. Going forward with the other guy will ruin it." Tears began to run down her face. She thanked me and left. A strong sense of satisfaction and elation overcame me for having performed this reading.

Two months later, I arrived at work one morning to find a gathering of women surrounding Rachel. Sure enough she was showing off her engagement ring. My reading had been exactly right on. What an empowering feeling to help people in need.

Broken Dreams

And as for Ann's reading for me—a great financial burden did indeed lift from Hailey and me—this sure did come true. We became so destitute and desperate we filed for bankruptcy! Hailey had been working three jobs and I two, yet we slipped further and further into debt. Hailey had even started a class in our home teaching kids some of the meditative techniques she knew, but too few kids enrolled—finally we admitted we were going under.

The bankruptcy erased a large portion of our debt but not all of it. As part of the legal agreement I had to give up my car. Now we were faced with still having to go to all of our jobs but with only one car. Both of us were frustrated, angry and depressed, and we did all we could do to blame one another for the situation in which we found ourselves.

Rarely a day passed that we didn't fight about something. The fights started about money but always ended with vicious personal attacks. At times I thought I was losing my mind. I had this feeling of being stirred up inside like someone else was saying those cruel words to Hailey. My anger and resentment toward Hailey seemed to be building momentum like an age-old dormant volcano ready to suddenly erupt. I behaved as if she was to blame for everything. But deep inside I felt tremendous guilt; as a man, I let my family down by not being responsible enough to just get a good paying job. Instead I put all my hopes on the universe or some lucky break that would lead us to wealth. My fragile ego wouldn't let me admit to her it was my fault.

When I discussed my situation with my classmates, we all agreed that the universe was teaching me a lesson, and I was to grow from it. This was the same universe that was telling me to hold on and everything would work out. Elinor explained to me, as she had many times, that I still had not truly let go and allowed the spirits to guide me. She told me I still struggled with trusting them. Again, it was all my fault. I couldn't help but feel betrayed by them though; I trusted them to guide me, and they guided me right to bankruptcy court. "This is a tough lesson for you Brian," Elinor reminded me. "Sometimes the universe has to hammer us to get our attention." Well, the universe had gotten my attention all right. Now what?

I continued performing readings to hone my skills. Each week in class, we all exchanged stories of how well our readings had gone or how much people appreciated them. Ann said she often felt the presence of her guides with her all the time. She said she enjoyed the voices in her head telling her what to do when she needed guidance; I experienced the same thing. Alison had decided to name each of hers as to keep track of who was who. We all thought that was pretty amusing and creative.

One evening, as I drove home from class the spirit guide who was the casual dresser spoke to me and said, *How about a name for me?* "What do you want to be named?" I asked out loud. *How about something easy, like Phil?* "Phil it is," I laughed. *What about me?* The gentle translucent one said. *I want the name Miriam. Is that okay?* She asked. "Miriam it is," I said. My two most frequently-used guides now had names—they were officially my *friends*.

The following week, June (my born-again friend and business colleague) and I scheduled a business presentation to do together, and we decided to meet for lunch to discuss the details. At one point during our conversation, June seemed to be troubled. "What's wrong?" I asked.

"Because I consider you a friend, Brian, I want to share with you what our family has been faced with in these last few months. We brought in a boarder who wished to work with us in our business. He seemed like a really good man, but we discovered he was molesting my eleven-year-old son." Her words shocked me.

"Oh my God, that's horrible," I exclaimed. She shared some of the disturbing details and the tremendous anguish this had caused her as a mother. "I never knew, I mean … you never let on that anything was wrong. How are you able to cope with all of this?" I asked.

"Reliance and trust in the Lord, Brian. Without the solid grounding I have in Christ, I don't think we could have handled this. When we were in pain, the Lord comforted us. When we called out to Him, He was there," she said as tears began to well up in her eyes. She collected herself and said, "I have never felt more strength in my faith than I have at this time in my life. This may not make sense to you Brian, but this challenge in our lives has brought us closer to the Lord. I know He lives." She said all this with more conviction than

I could have believed possible to have.

After lunch she gave me a hug and said, "Brian, the Lord is there for you also." I didn't respond. I just said thanks and got into my car. Her story really shook me up. I was disturbed that someone would do that to a child, but I was amazed at her attitude of trust and peace. She actually was able to forgive this guy. She said she did not despair—she knew God was going to take care of things and she could let go of the anger and accept God's healing. How could anyone do that?

The following week after we had completed our presentation, I shared with June the results of my last reading. I was so excited about it because it had gone so well. As I unfolded the story to her, the expression on her face began to change from one of calmness to sheer anxiety. She looked like I had just told her I had terminal cancer. She said nothing, but she had fear written all over. *Why is this scaring her*, I wondered. *What is it she is afraid of?* That moment hung with me for days afterwards.

I was feeling quite distraught about my relationship with Hailey, and I wanted so much to resolve our differences and make our life together better. One evening, I asked Ann to perform a reading for me, secretly hoping for some solid answers.

She ran her energy and then gave me information about my job and money but nothing about Hailey. I finally asked what the future was going to be for Hailey and me. She paused and then said, "There doesn't seem to be a clear answer about this right now. I'm sorry."

Two weeks later Hailey asked me for a divorce. I never even saw it coming. No matter how bad things got I had never considered giving up. She said she didn't want to live like this any longer.

A week later she moved out. We put the house up for sale, and I stayed with the house for the next two months until it sold. It was the loneliest two months of my life. My heart felt like it had shattered in a million pieces, not to mention my self-confidence that had gone down the drain too.

Now having to find work and a place to live without a car and being without much money, I had what seemed like the insurmountable task of putting my life back together. I had been working part-time as a customer-service representative for a health-care company and was fortunate that a position opened to go full time. One of the supervisors was looking for a roommate to help pay the bills for his condominium. Although I didn't know him well, he lived nearby, and we could ride to work together.

Everyone called my new roommate Big Al. He was a 6' 5" tall black guy with a great jovial sense of humor. We became fast friends, and I was lucky to have a place to live.

At work, my ability to perform readings gained me a reputation. I would do a reading on anyone who showed any interest at all. One evening, my roommate dropped me off at a friend's apartment. Julie wanted me to perform a reading. I ran my energy and answered several questions for her—she said I was very accurate. Julie was single and was looking for the right man to come into her life. I told her the man of her dreams I saw was wearing a white lab coat. I wasn't sure if that meant a doctor or perhaps a lab technician, but she was pretty excited about that. She had one last person to ask me about, a friend for whom she had much concern. "Could you tell me how she is doing?" Julie pleaded.

Miriam whispered, *I'll show you a picture.* I saw a cartoonish figure made out of paper, and it looked like a child had made it. This paper cut out of the woman was colored in crayon, and the paper was crumpled and damaged.

"Is your friend sick, or is she hurt in some way?" I asked Julie. Becoming distressed, she paused, then said, "Yes, she has cancer. I want to know if she is going to live." This was one of those questions that I needed to be careful how to answer.

Miriam said, *Watch, and you will have the answer.*

The scene I beheld in my mind grew very dark except for a spotlight pouring down on an empty stage. Then a woman appeared singing a sad and mournful song. She then faded from view, but her voice could still be heard. The scene changed to a small calm pond at night. Mist hung above the dark water as a black swan swam across in front of me. The woman's voice sang lower and lower as her tone filled with the emotion of pain and anguish. The swan cruised through the water creating a small wake and then little by little disappeared beneath the surface of the water. The woman stopped singing, and the pond became empty. The image was easy to understand—Julie's friend was going to die.

I looked above Julie's head, and the rose appeared standing upright. "I'm sorry Julie, but I don't think she is going to make it." Julie nodded silently and said, "I was afraid you were going to say that. Her doctors haven't given her much of a chance either." Julie thanked me for my time and drove me home. Two weeks later she told me her friend had died. As painful as this reading had been for me to give Julie, I knew in my heart I had done a good thing. It was certainly helping people with their lives, their sorrows and their challenges. *And if it is helping people*, I reasoned, *it must be good*. Thus I had no intention of ending these readings and my dealings with my spirit guides. I knew if something seemed this good, it must be so.

More Than Just an Experience

"Hey Brian, why don't you come to church sometime." It was June on the other end of the line. Although performing readings was great, I was at the lowest point in my life. I had lost my wife, my house, my car, and I was living in a small condo with a guy I hardly knew. Even still, June's offer didn't sound too appealing as I had heard plenty about the church she attended, and one of the things I heard was that it was a fundamentalist type church. But on the other hand, June had been so kind to me—how could I say no? So before I knew what I was saying, I agreed to go with her. When I hung up, I thought, *Why in the world did I agree to go?*

I was surprised by the appearance of Village Community Church. For one thing, it was the largest church I had ever been in. The spire on top of the church could be seen for miles. I was used to Catholic churches, dimly lit with dark wood and stained glass. Village Community was brightly lit with white walls, blond oak trim, and on top of that everyone seemed so happy. I chose a seat in the balcony as far back as possible so no one would bother me or try to get me to join. I wanted to be anonymous—listen and then get out of there as fast as I could.

As I waited for the service to begin, my eyes traveled from one end of the place to the other, carefully examining each person. I was very curious about the people and secretly hoped I could spot some peculiarity about them. Most of them dressed fashionably, and I didn't see one woman wearing gingham. As a matter of fact, they looked so … normal, considering I had heard they were narrow-minded fundamentalists. What was the real story behind the facade?

As a musician, I had really learned to pick out good music, and I was surprised at the quality of the music and the musicians. They played hymns with a contemporary beat. I had not heard music like this in a church since basic training in the Air Force, and I had never heard a rock-style lead guitar playing a hymn before. What really took me by surprise though was the sermon. Pastor Scott Miller didn't just read out of the Bible. He made the Bible relevant in these times and to my life right then. He used references to today's world that I could relate to. After the service was over, I had to admit this was the most pleasant experience I had ever had going to church. I really enjoyed it. Yet I wasn't about to tell June that! Shrugging my shoulders, showing as little interest as possible, I told her I might come back again.

One week blended into the next, and I continued going to Village Community. A clear message rang out in every sermon—the God of the Bible was real, and He wanted to have a relationship with me. Somehow, I didn't feel threatened that I wasn't good enough to be at this church, and I was amazed to see the people at this church taking their faith so seriously. This was the essence of their lives, and they really lived this life everyday, not just on Sunday.

I had never met Christians like this. I was impressed, and I began noticing something they had that I did not … peace and a sense of satisfaction and direction in their lives. Each week someone stood up in front of the congregation and shared his or her testimony of how Jesus changed their life. Many times I felt moved to tears by these stories. Could Jesus really be the answer? I had held so much prejudice against Christians. I really could not conceive becoming one of them. That really would be unthinkable. I would never be able to give up my lifestyle and be such a goody-goody person all the time. I still had the rock 'n' roll bad boy inside, and that wasn't going to magically disappear. However, a powerful sense of loneliness inside and the feeling I had of being incomplete began to surface. After years of being able to stuff such feelings into a box that was neatly wrapped with rock 'n' roll, drugs, alcohol and sex, I suddenly found them pushing at the seams of my mind trying to jump out at me from every direction.

I had one nagging question though—*how can I know for sure if all the stories about Jesus are true? The Bible was written so long ago and mistranslated so many times how can anyone believe this?* I considered myself to be a logical, analytical person. I was not into this blind faith, which these Christians believed.

Surprised by Evidence

In April, I moved out of Al's place and found a place with my friend Maurice from the band. He had recently gone through a divorce, and he too needed a roommate. He and I had always gotten along great, and it was nice to be living with an old friend.

I no sooner got unpacked and settled, when June stopped by to tell me about a special speaker at Village Community. "You've got to hear this guy," she said with a hint of enthusiasm. She knew she needed to be careful about not coming on too strong, or I'd be running in the opposite direction. "This guy is a scientist who became a Christian after examining the evidence that supports the historical accuracy of the Bible."

"That's a mouthful, June. You sure about all that? You sure this guy is an actual scientist? I've never heard of a Christian scientist before—sounds like an oxymoron."

Without saying much more, June handed me a brochure about the meeting. "Hmmm. Dr. Don Bierle, eh?" Well, he certainly had the credentials—an M.A. and Ph.D. in the life sciences and an M.A. in New Testament studies. He had also been a college professor for 25 years. *What a contrast,* I thought. Something didn't compute. How could someone be a scientist and a Christian at the same time? *This I've got to see!* I had no question in my mind that any *evidence* he produced would indeed *not* be evidence but would still demand a blind faith attitude.

The three-part seminar was held at Village Community three Sunday nights in a row. I was sure I could ask the tough questions and Dr. Bierle would not be able to answer them. I could hardly wait to stump this guy. I could put him in his place right in front of everyone. *That'll teach him to go around boasting of such claims.*

The atmosphere at the church that night had been transformed into more of a college-class lecture than a church service. I was expecting singing, alleluias and amens—but none of that took place. Dr. Bierle began the first night destroying most of my arguments about the Bible mistranslations and the chance for inaccuracies. He explained how a historian would examine any ancient writing. First he would investigate how many manuscript copies have been found. Don shared how more than 5,664 known manuscripts of the New Testament in the original Greek language exist, with an additional 18,000 ancient manuscripts in Latin, Syriac, Armenian and other language versions. In addition, when such texts as ancient hymn books are included, more than 24,000 handwritten copies of portions of the New Testament have survived. In contrast, merely ten manuscripts of Caesar's *The Gallic Wars*, seven of Plato's *Tetralogies*, twenty for Livy's *History of Rome*, and two of Tacitus's minor works have survived.[1] Yet these works are accepted without question.

He pointed out how the number of New Testament manuscripts in existence from before the invention of the printing press far outnumbers other ancient works. He sounded convincing; yet as far as I was concerned, this alone did not prove the accuracy of the Bible.

Next Dr. Bierle discussed the time interval between the date the apostles penned their writings and the earliest known manuscript of the New Testament compared to other ancient works. Don writes in his book *Surprised By Faith:*

> How close to the authorship do archaeologists actually find ancient manuscript copies? Caesar's *Gallic Wars* was authored about 50 B.C., yet we have no manuscripts available for study today which were copied before the ninth century—a gap of over 900 years. Most of the Greek writings have even greater gaps (1,000-1,500 years), while the Latin works have somewhat less. The shortest span of any generally accepted ancient work is

*This section from *Surprised by Faith*, by Dr. Don Bierle, is used by permission.

probably that of Virgil, about 300 years between his authorship and the oldest known copy. However, such a short time period is not at all typical. People are troubled when they discover that there are no preserved copies of classical works for hundreds of years after the date of original composition. But they are astonished when they see the data concerning the New Testament.

It is generally agreed that the 27 books and letters of the New Testament were penned over a fifty-year period, beginning approximately A.D. 47. For ease in calculations, I will use the year A.D. 100 as the latest possible date for their completion. What is the earliest copy ever found? Remember, the range for all other literature is 300 to more than 1,500 years after authorship. The John Ryland's papyrus, designated by scholars as P52, is a fragment containing a few verses of the New Testament Gospel of John, dating about A.D. 125. This is only some 35 years after the original Gospel had been written by the apostle. Whoever used this copy could have known the author, or even been personally taught by the apostle John, himself.

Furthermore, a strong case has been made recently by Dr. Young Kyu Kim, a manuscript scholar, that the Chester Beatty Papyrus (P46), containing all of Paul's epistles except the pastorals, should be re-dated to the late first century. This is only about twenty years after the apostle died!

But that's not all. Studies of the late-first and early-second century extant writings of those who were students of the eyewitness apostles (e.g., Polycarp, Clement of Rome, Ignatius) reveal extensive references to New Testament writings. For example, about A.D. 96, Clement of Rome refers to the Gospels of Matthew, Mark and Luke, and eight other New

Testament letters. Obviously, they must have been written some time before that date in order for Clement to site them.

Supporting that conclusion are the recently analyzed fragments of Matthew (Magdalen Papyrus), a scroll fragment of Mark at Qumran, and a papyrus fragment of Luke in a Paris library that have been dated by some scholars between A.D. 50 and A.D. 70. Since Jesus lived at least until A.D. 30, these copies were made by people who were contemporaries of Jesus—people who knew Him personally or talked with those who did. While these three manuscripts are all fragments, they nevertheless demonstrate that the Gospels were in written form very early. They did not go through a long period of oral transmission during which they took on legendary traditions. No other ancient writing can trace its manuscript copies all the way back to the generation of the eyewitnesses and its original authors![2]

I wondered though how accurately the manuscripts had been copied. The answer to this question would measure the extent of distortion of the text due to copying over the centuries:

Dr. Bruce Metzger, professor of New Testament language and literature at Princeton published an analysis on this very question. He compared research into the many manuscripts of three ancient works: Homer's *Iliad*, a religious work of the ancient Greeks; the *Mahabharata*, a religious book of Hinduism; and the Christian New Testament. The works varied in length from 15,600 lines for the *Iliad*, 20,000 for the New Testament, and 250,000 for the *Mahabharata*. Variations such as spelling differences, word order, etc., that did not affect the meaning of the text were ignored. All differences in the manuscripts affecting the reader's understanding were counted. How much distortion did he find?

Dr. Metzger summarized that 764 lines of the *Iliad* were corrupted, a distortion rate of about 5%. Said another way, the meaning of one out of every twenty lines is uncertain. Which *Iliad* do we read in literature class? Who decided which ancient manuscript is the correct one? Yet, it is probably rare that an instructor would caution students about the integrity of the *Iliad* when it is assigned or discussed in class. Its integrity is assumed without question.

The *Mahabharata* is even worse with at least 26,000 lines corrupted, somewhat more than a 10% distortion rate. One out of every ten lines of this religious book was "up for grabs," so to speak. This is not a very reliable source on which to base your life or your destiny!

The data for the New Testament, on the other hand, is incredible. Only 40 of 20,000 lines, or 1/5 of 1%, are distorted. This is 1/25th of the distortion found in the *Iliad*, which itself has a low distortion rate among ancient writings. Further, F.F. Bruce has said that "the variant readings about which any doubt remains among textual critics of the New Testament affect no material question of historic fact or of Christian faith and practice." Said more simply, no teaching of the Christian faith is in question as a result of the distortion of the New Testament text due to copying over many centuries.[3]

At the end of the first class, I was impressed but disturbed. I had no idea this type of information existed. I could hardly believe that historical evidence supported the authenticity of the Bible. I had entered this class so confident that I could challenge Dr. Bierle, and he would fold with the well-you-just-have-to-believe line. But I was wrong. He had the evidence, and all I had was my arrogance.

The second class built upon the first, citing more evidence and bringing me to the edge of a deep ravine, a ravine I had refused to face—could it be that the Bible was historically reliable? My objections to the Bible were crumbling like century-old buildings in a massive earthquake. As I left the class, one question permeated my thoughts … and my heart—could the story of Jesus be true? As I headed home I didn't think I even wanted to know the answer to that question. If it were true, my whole view of the world would suddenly change. Everything I stood for, everything I lived for would crumble. I knew it, and I couldn't bear the thought.

Waking Up From a Long, Lost Dream

I asked June to come with me to the last class. During the session, Don told a story from the Bible that really shook me. The story was about Abraham and his desire to have a son. God had promised him a son, but the years went by, and he and his wife Sarah were getting old. Sarah was well past her childbearing years. However, when she was ninety and Abraham was one hundred God blessed them with a son whom Abraham named Isaac. God then tested Abraham's faith and asked him to take his beloved son into the land of Moriah and sacrifice him. Abraham traveled many miles to arrive at the place God had instructed him to go to sacrifice his one and only son. Abraham brought his son up the hill to set him upon the altar, and not until Abraham raised the knife to slay his son did God cry out, "Do not lay your hand on the lad, or do anything to him; for now I know that you fear God, since you have not withheld your son, your only son, from Me" (Genesis 22:12). God knew that Abraham was willing to obey God even in such a difficult circumstance. Don then told us that the very same place where Isaac was to be sacrificed, 2000 years later on the same hillside, the Jewish Temple was built, and that was the same hillside where Jesus would hang on the Cross.

I realized there was no way this could be a coincidence. Abraham was to sacrifice his one and only son on the same hillside where God's son would be sacrificed 2000 years later? The last block of my unbelief was suddenly shattered. It was true. The story of Jesus was true! For the first time in my life, I knew it was true. June and I sat in the back of the classroom as I prayed for God's forgiveness. Right there and then I accepted Jesus as my personal Savior and asked Him to come into my heart and make me born-again. June's eyes welled up with tears as she put her arm around me. "Am I really a Christian now?" I asked.

She smiled and said, "Do you believe Jesus is Lord?"

"Yes," I replied.

"Then you are a Christian; you are a child of God, and you are forgiven," she said with joy beyond her imagination.

As I stood to leave, I felt a little dizzy and disoriented. I hugged her and thanked her for being there with me. I walked out to the parking lot towards my car, when suddenly Phil's voice entered my mind and said, *You are not a Christian, Brian. You just said some words. You can't be a Christian!* Phil sounded different. He sounded angry and disturbed. *You can't live like that. You are not going to be able to be good for the rest of your life. You are kidding yourself.* His words echoed in my head until I fell asleep that night. Was I really a Christian?

After I got home from work the following day, I stopped by the liquor store and decided to pick up some beer. This was unusual for me. I was not a big drinker and I rarely, if ever, drank at home. Sitting alone in my darkened living room, I drank a few beers, and then I did something I had never done before—I got in my car and drove to a video store to rent some porn videos. I had never rented one before. I had certainly seen them in the Air Force and at some bachelor parties, but I had never rented any ever before.

I felt really creepy about getting them. I always pictured someone who rented them to be desperately lonely and pathetic, and I wasn't sure why I was doing this. I picked some out and headed home. I watched them and drank more beer. The next day, I was hung over and decided to call in sick to work. I slept on the couch in the morning and then later got up in the afternoon to return the videos and get some more beer. As I drove to the liquor store, I questioned why I was behaving this way? Miriam purred in my head, *"Do you really want to give this life up?"* I pushed her voice out of my head. I grabbed another six-pack and instead of dropping off the videos, I decided to rent more.

When I got in line, a woman and a child stood in front of me. The mother looked at the video in my hand and smirked, drawing her child closer to her as if I was some evil villain waiting to lurch out and attack her child. I felt my face redden with embarrassment and shame, but it didn't stop me. Without making eye contact with the man at the cash register, I paid for the videos and drove home. All that afternoon and into the evening I watched videos and continued to drink. At the end of the night, I crawled into bed tired and drunk. Phil spoke sharply, condemning me, *Do you see what I mean? You are not a Christian. This is the way you are, and you are not going to change. We didn't make you drink, Brian— you chose to do it all on your own.*

I fell into a deep sleep until my alarm woke me in the morning. My head pounded as I lifted it off the pillow, and I knew there was no way I could go to work. I again called in sick.

I went downstairs and collapsed on the couch. I felt bad from the hangover, but something else far deeper was bothering me. *Why am I acting this way? Why did I rent those videos and get drunk two days in a row? Aren't I supposed to be Christian now? Why at this time? This isn't like me.* The voices of my guides were constantly ringing in my head. Of all the philosophies and religions I had looked into and considered, I never felt this type of resistance or opposition from my guides. In fact, I often felt an urging from my guides to further pursue and study Buddhism and Hinduism. What was so different about Christianity?

And then I saw it! The answer came to me in an instant. As if a veil was lifted from my eyes, I saw something I had never seen before. The reason they were resisting me was because they were opposed to Him. They hated Jesus. All at once every memory of anything anyone had ever said about Jesus, Satan and demons came flooding into my mind. And I realized my guides were opposed to Jesus, because they were demonic. They did not want me to become a Christian, because they were not of God. Satan, in his attempt to keep me where I was, revealed who *he* was! In order to stop me, he had revealed himself to me. He was now exposed. His real identity and the identity of my guides were revealed.

"My God," I cried out loud. I fell to my knees and began to cry, "Oh my God, my Lord, I have been wrong my entire life! You are the truth. You are the way. Please Jesus save me. Please God forgive me for I have sinned against you." I crawled into a ball and wept like a child.

From that moment on I knew who God was. The truth had been revealed to me. Jesus Christ is Lord, and I am saved. Amen!!

In the weeks and months that followed I began to learn about the Bible, but this time I read it with joy and excitement. I found God's book exhilarating, knowing it was the truth. When I went to church I went with great enthusiasm. Several times when singing, I began to weep, knowing what the Lord had done for me. He had set me free. For the first time in my life I knew who the Father was, who I was and then very soon what plans He had for my life. Is that not the answer every human being wishes to know? In one instant, I knew what truth was. I felt the peace in my heart and in my head that I had seen in other Christians. It's a peace and assurance that has never left me to this day.

Framework of a Strange Religion

A s folks at Village Community Church learned of my conversion, many asked me to share my story with others. As time passed, such requests became more frequent. Everyone seemed very interested in hearing how a former New Ager found Christ. I soon realized though how very little I really knew about the New Age. It seemed rather ironic—now that I was a Christian and no longer into the New Age, I now needed to learn all I could about this belief system. I not only wanted to warn my new brothers and sisters about the New Age movement, but my heart yearned to share my new faith with my old friends, hoping to convince them Jesus truly is Lord. Thus began my research into the heart and soul of the New Age movement, a religious belief system encased in a framework that opposes the very nature of Jesus Christ.

Delving into the origins of the practices I had performed, I found it disconcerting to discover the practice of *running my energy* was a form of witchcraft. In a book by Peter Jones, *Spirit Wars*, Dr. Jones shares what he describes as a witchcraft or goddess worship style of meditation taught at *The Parliament of the World's Religions* conference. The Isis group at the conference led a group of women in this meditation:

> Bring that energy up, up through your roots, into your body. Let it come in through the soles of your feet, rise up your body, all the way to your fingertips. That energy can handle whatever comes to you. All you need to do is to call it up. Feel the power of that energy. Now allow that energy to spiral around your spinal column, rising ... and then allow the energy to sprout

out your head as branches ... Feel your connection
with the other women in the circle.[1]

I found striking similarities between this meditation and the
one I practiced. I was shocked. Here I thought I was engaging in a
meditation that brought me into unity with the Universe; in reality
I had practiced a form of witchcraft.

One Saturday afternoon, a couple of years after I became a Christian, Hailey came to my apartment to discuss some leftover financial
matters. By now I had moved out of Maurice's apartment into a place
of my own. It had taken me over a year to pay off the debt left over
from our marriage, and I was finally back on my feet financially.

Hailey knew I had become a Christian and seemed a little uncomfortable being around me. She teased me about being one of those *born-agains*, and yet she seemed curious as to how this happened to me.

Wanting her reaction to my discovery in Peter Jones' book, I asked
her about the class and the meditations we performed to run our
energy. I read the paragraph from Jones' book and asked, "Did you
know the practice we were involved in was witchcraft?"

She laughed and said, "Brian, I *am* a witch."

I was surprised at her answer.

"You didn't know that? I used to say it all the time."

"I thought you were joking," I answered, staring in disbelief as
I sat on the couch across the room from her.

"No, I wasn't. In fact I am now involved in Wicca." From
what I had come to know, Wicca was just a politically correct name
for witchcraft.

I tried to share with her my joy in discovering the truth about
Christ, but she immediately responded, "You mean *your* truth."

I was getting a little taste of my own medicine; how many times
had I said that very thing to well-meaning Christians? "Only one
truth exists, Hailey. Either the story of Jesus is true, or it is not."

"Even still, that is what you believe to be truth," she shot back.
We had learned this line well together.

We argued back and forth about the existence of one truth. I finally asked her, "Did O. J. Simpson kill his wife or not?" She gave me a puzzled look. "He either did it, or he didn't. The answer is not both. Right? He didn't both kill her and at the same time *not* kill her. Isn't that correct?" Hailey didn't answer. I was on a roll, so I continued, "That question has only one true answer. Some may have different opinions about it, but it did happen only one way."

"What does this have to do with God?" she asked.

I continued, feeling as though I really had her ear now. "A God who has the characteristics of personage listens, loves, and cares. However, an impersonal God can be described like the wind or electricity. It exists, perhaps it has power, you can feel it, but it can't love, listen or care. God can't be both personal and impersonal at the same time. It is either one or the other but not both. God is either a who or an it, right?"

Hailey looked at me, and for one short instant, I could see by the expression on her face that my logical point had pierced her thoughts. However, the moment didn't last long. Her expression immediately turned to one of defiance. "So of course *you* are right, and *everyone* else is wrong?"

Softening my voice, I said, "There is only one truth about God, and the consequences for rejecting the truth are detrimental, Hailey."

Saying that made her angry, and I knew the reaction all too well from my own years of struggle. "So, I suppose I am going to Hell?" she asked in a sarcastic tone.

"I just want you to consider that the story of Jesus is true," I said emphatically.

She got up and walked toward the door. "I don't need any of this." As she reached the door, she turned and said, "I suppose after I leave, you are going to pray for me, right?"

I smiled at her and answered, "Yes."

She responded with defiance, "Don't bother. My mother prays for me all of the time, and it doesn't make any difference. I have enough people praying for me." With that, she turned and walked out.

I've thought about that conversation for many years, struck by the change in her demeanor after she contemplated my point. For a moment the wheels turned in her mind as she realized it was impossible for God to be both personal and impersonal at the same time. I soon realized that New Agers base everything upon the experiential. Do not *think* about anything or intellectually challenge anything. Accept everything that feels good, no matter if it makes little or no sense. Logic, reason and thinking are an anathema to the New Ager. Feelings and emotions guide all decisions in life.

For a brief moment, Hailey broke the rules of the New Age. She committed a *sin* according to a postmodernist—she pondered the possibility of a right and wrong answer, considering for just a moment that perhaps only one truth about God exists.

What are the belief systems of the New Age? Why are they so popular? Who are the gurus? And where do they get all these ideas? If you are a New Ager, I ask you to continue with me here and learn what it really means to be a New Ager. If you are not a New Ager but rather a Christian, you may be in for the surprise of your life because this very New Age movement I speak of has and is now infiltrating the Christian church at a rapid and alarming rate. And you can imagine my horror when I left the New Age movement only to find the very same techniques and practices I literally ran from were waiting patiently for me in the church pews, pulpits and bookstores of the church. Oh, it isn't called the New Age movement—names have been changed. But as a rose by any other name is just as sweet so too is the New Age movement by any other name just as deviant and dangerous. And there's a very good chance it has already entered your church, your college and even your home.

Key Elements of the New Age

The New Age is a rather complex subject combining Occultism, Hinduism, Buddhism, Humanism, Paganism and more. The remainder of this chapter gives a basic outline of some of the more prominent and popular practices and ph not comprehensive by any means, it certainly pre ture of the New Age framework:

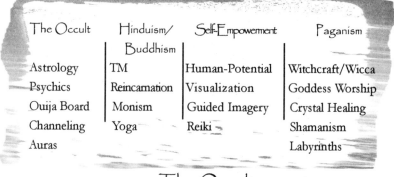

The Occult	Hinduism/ Buddhism	Self-Empowerment	Paganism
Astrology	TM	Human-Potential	Witchcraft/Wicca
Psychics	Reincarnation	Visualization	Goddess Worship
Ouija Board	Monism	Guided Imagery	Crystal Healing
Channeling	Yoga	Reiki	Shamanism
Auras			Labyrinths

The Occult

Astrology

Astrology is the belief that events on Earth correspond to the positions and movements of astronomical bodies, particularly the sun, moon, planets, and stars. "Astrologers believe the position of astronomical bodies at the exact moment of a person's birth and the subsequent movements of the bodies reflect that person's character and, therefore, destiny."[2] However, there is one problem; it has never been proven to be accurate as far as predicting events or shaping one's personality. Many thousands of people look up their horoscopes in the newspaper each day, but what they really should be doing is seeking guidance from the God who created the planets and the One who set them in motion.

Psychics and Mediums

Those who practice utilizing mental or supernatural powers to predict the future or to gain insights into the present circumstances of the world constitute psychics or mediums. As well, mediums attempt to contact or communicate with spirit guides or the dead.

It is clear from Scripture that God forbids this:

> There shall not be found among you anyone who makes his son or his daughter pass through the fire, or one who practices witchcraft, or a soothsayer, or one who interprets

omens, or a sorcerer, or one who conjures spells, or a medium, or a spiritist, or one who calls up the dead. For all who do these things are an abomination to the LORD. (Deuteronomy 18: 10-12)

Ouija Board

Invented in Baltimore in 1892, it is trademark for a board bearing the alphabet and various symbols with a planchette that is moved by the fingers to spell out messages, supposedly under the direction of spirits.[3] I, like many people, played with this *game* when I was a kid. I remember my sister playing with a Ouija board with her friends, and the spirit communicating with them claimed to be living in *Middle Earth;* his name was George. They all laughed at his reference and saw the game as a great way to have fun. However, playing this game opens a door to communicating with spirits. As innocent and harmless as it may seem, it is anything but that.

Channeling

Similar to psychic readings, channeling engages the use of communicating with spirit guides. However, instead of communication with the dead, it is communication with an *ascended master or spirit being.* The channeler is used as a vehicle for the spirit through which to communicate. "The controlling spirit or entity will lecture, counsel, teach, or otherwise advise its human audience through these channelers."[4] One channeler described this technique as the ability to communicate with very powerful beings who give insight into the world and future changes to prepare for. Many channelers give vague warnings, telling people to protect themselves from various energies coming into the planet that may disrupt plans. Often channelers try to predict investment opportunities.

At times this channeling seems like a psychic weather report:

> *Don't forget to wear your cosmic raincoat as the negative energy flowing from the east may cause you to blow your savings on a frivolous venture.*

Auras

A radiant *glow* or energy field that supposedly emanates from and surrounds all living things is an aura. It is not perceived by ordinary vision but by clairvoyance. Although no evidence has been found to prove its existence, the concept has thrived as a pseudoscience. During my training to become a medium, I spent time attempting to read the auras of classmates and of others. Although I personally never saw anything surrounding anyone's body, I did sense someone's feeling or mood by concentrating as if I saw an aura. In retrospect, I realize I was using the method used by every human being on the planet—the power of observation. If your co-worker's voice seems lower and slower and her movements seem lethargic and you notice she doesn't want to smile, could it be she is depressed? Could it be that something is bothering her? Wow, how did you know that? You must obviously have some hidden powers!

Hinduism/Buddhism

Transcendental Meditation (TM)

TM or Transcendental Meditation is a religious movement that was founded by Maharishi Mahesh Yogi and brought from India to the West in 1959. When Maharishi's predecessor, Guru Dev of India, died in 1953, Maharishi went into seclusion for two years. He then emerged to found the International Academy of Meditation near the Himalayas. There he developed a strategy to spread TM around the globe. From then on he was called Maharishi (meaning 'great sage') Mahesh (his family name) Yogi (meaning: *united with God*).[5] The practice became quite popular in the 1960s, attracting well-knowns such as "actress Mia Farrow, cultural philosopher Marshall McLuhan, and the Beatles who eventually rejected the Yogi's teachings."[6]

The focus of TM is on meditation and the sensual pleasures the practice brings while aiding individuals in reaching a unique level of consciousness or an altered state of consciousness. The technique involves the repeating of a word called a mantra over and over again in your mind until you reach a silence or a silencing of all thoughts. This is believed to be a state of nirvana where the stresses of life can be reduced. The technique is practiced twice daily for fifteen to twenty minutes, once upon rising and once in the evening. During this technique, your mind may wander to other thoughts, but you are instructed to acknowledge the thought and then let it drift away as you repeat the mantra again and again. After a period of time, fewer and fewer thoughts remain, and then the repeating of the mantra disappears. The goal of this exercise is to be rid of all thoughts and allow the mind to go into a type of neutral state.

TM is actually not new but was practiced in ancient Hinduism and Brahmanism as devotion to the impersonal *God*, Brahman, through various forms of *yoga*. The Maharishi recommends *bhakti yoga* as his preferred choice, where devotion is displayed by elevating the mind from ordinary thought to an altered state of consciousness. The world is merely *Maya* or an illusion, and consequently the real world is found in *cosmic consciousness*—a state of perfect rest.

It is evident, therefore, that TM is more than just a religious exercise, but an all-encompassing philosophy of life, a philosophy that denies the validity of the real world while making the world of illusion the reality. Futhermore, since illusion has no structure or limits, there is no telling where the path of illusion will take someone. It is unbridled and unprotected mental thought that provides a perfect avenue for a demonic spirit world to intercept and redirect our way of thinking.

Reincarnation

The belief of the cyclical return of a soul to live another life in a new body is called reincarnation. I like to call it soul recycling. Reincarnation offers the false hope of a continued existence in other lives thus providing ongoing chances to reach perfection and freedom. This belief system is in dire opposition to the Christian teaching that the soul of man lives once and has a day of final judgment with the possibility of being eternally condemned to suffer in Hell. One explanation why reincarnation is so popular states:

> [I]t allegedly explains the differences that exist between
> people. Some are healthy, others are tormented their
> whole life by physical handicaps. Some are rich, others
> at the brink of starvation. Some have success without
> being religious; others are constant losers despite their
> religious dedication. Eastern religions explain these
> differences as a result of previous lives, good or bad,
> which bear their fruits into the present one through the
> action of karma. Therefore reincarnation seems to be a
> perfect way of punishing or rewarding one's deeds
> without the need of accepting a personal God as
> Ultimate Reality.[7]

Scripture refutes reincarnation when it says in Hebrews 9:27, "And as it is appointed for men to die once, but after this the judgment." And in Jesus' parable of Lazarus and the rich man (Luke 16:20), we learn that Lazarus was seated next to Abraham in Heaven after having lived only once; the rich man, on the other hand, found himself in Hell after having lived only once. Notice too, that Lazarus, who was poor and sickly during his life, found himself next to Abraham in his death—a highly prestigious position according to Hebrew tradition. Whatever happened to his bad karma? The rich man, on the other hand, who supposedly had a good karma during his life, having evolved to higher virtues in successive lifetimes, now finds himself in Hell. Is it possible that God has a different view of things than the scenario reincarnation suggests?

Monism

Monism is a Hindu belief that all is one, and one is all. I explain it this way: You and the chair you sit on, the ground on which it stands and the Earth underneath is all one. "I am that, you are that, all this is that and that is all there is" (Hindu Proverb). Monism does not distinguish between God and man and even nature.

Yoga

Yoga has its roots in Hinduism and is widely practiced by Hindu and Buddhist monks. The word itself is Sanskrit and means *to unite*. Some of the major yoga systems include Karma, Hatha, and Kundalini. In the Western world Yoga has become almost a household name. While many try to say Yoga is not a religious belief system but rather just a form of health and exercise, anyone doing even a brief study on the framework of Yoga will easily be convinced this is a religious belief that teaches how all of humanity shares a Godlike potential which unites us all. According to John Newport, author of *The New Age Movement and the Biblical Worldview*, "spiritual discipline is the best translation of the term [Yoga]."

A simple word search on Google during the past two years shows a phenomenal growth in the popularity of Yoga. In 2002, there were approximately 1.2 million web pages carrying the term Yoga. Today, just 26 months later, that number has neared 20 million. Ignoring exponential growth, at the current rate, in five years, there will be 800 million web pages. Now granted this is not a scientific approach for projecting, but it certainly can paint a picture of where the world is going.

Patanjali, in his *Yoga Sutras* (I.2), says, "Yoga is the restraining of the mind-stuff (*chitta*) from taking various forms (*vrittis*)." Swami Yogananda, one of the most respected gurus to arrive in America (1920), termed yoga the "science of mind control." "Yoga," he wrote, "is a method for restraining the natural turbulence of thoughts, which otherwise impartially prevents all men, of all lands, from glimpsing their true nature of Spirit." In the same book, he further clarifies this definition: "yoga, 'union,' science of uniting the individual soul with the Cosmic Spirit." This certainly sounds like a religious practice to me.[8]

Sadly, many are trying and succeeding in bringing Yoga into the church. Why do Christians need a pagan practice brought into the church? Whenever I run into skepticism by Christians who practice Yoga I ask them these questions, "Do you believe that people living in India who are practicing Yoga (and those who practiced Yoga in India for many past centuries) are doing to it get *rock hard abs?* Do you think they are doing it to relieve the stress of a forty-hour work week? No, of course not. They are doing it because it is a religious practice in which they believe unifies them with Brahmin (Creator).

Self-Empowerment

Human Potential Movement

The Human Potential movement is a branch of psychology based on the belief that every human being has untapped and unrealized potential. Its goal is to help individuals achieve self-realization utilizing Freudian and Gestalt psychology in various therapy settings. Meditative and self-help guru techniques are incorporated into this program as an aid to reaching ultimate potential with the underlying premise being that every individual is God or God-like.

Creative Visualization/Guided Imagery

Creative Visualization is the practice of creating mental images for the purpose of self-improvement or personal gain. The underlying belief is that if someone can create a mental picture of a desired outcome—let's say more confidence in social and business settings, or a physical healing—then that outcome can be achieved by mentally picturing it into existence. Here again is the underlying philosophy that every human being has a higher self or the *God* within who can, like God, virtually speak things into existence.

Within the New Age movement, the practice of creative visualization is usually identified with Shakti Gawain, who got her start working for Ken Keyes's *Living Love Center* in Berkeley, California in the 1970s. Her workshops led to the writing of the book, *Creative Visualization.* Creative visualization, when "properly performed, requires contacting a 'higher self' and 'coming from the 'source.'" And 'source,' Gawain declares, 'means the supply of infinite love, wisdom and energy in the universe.""[9] The belief is that our thoughts can actually manifest occurrences in life. What we believe, we can conceive—in essence, we create our own reality.

What is the difference between using our imagination and creative visualization? If I was on the golf course and was summing up the next shot in my mind, is there something wrong with that? Of course not. If I think to myself and visualize my back swing to be just enough to get the ball on the green is that wrong? No. However, creative visualization surpasses the limits of a healthy imagination and purports that you can make the golf ball go where you want by the power of your mind. Creative visualization manipulates the world and reality.

Here is another example. A young man of seventeen is about to ask out the prettiest girl in school. He practices in his mind, "Hi Cindy, how are you today? Are you busy this Friday night? Would you like to go to a movie ... ahhh with me? Ahhh ... no that's not right." He tries different ways of practicing until it is right. He may also say to himself, "Be cool and calm, you will be okay. Everything will be fine."

The teen is merely practicing in his mind the desired outcome of his speech, helping to build his confidence—nothing wrong with that. However, with creative visualization the boy would say, "I see Cindy saying yes to me. I see her feeling drawn to me. She will feel tremendously attracted to me."

Coupled with the practice of creative visualization is the use of spirit guides. According to Shakti Gawain, creative visualization can easily introduce the practitioner to *"spirit guides*, the likes of which would be thrilled to meet us."[10]

Guided Imagery is in the same category as creative visualization. However, it is a process of visualization that is usually assisted by someone else or by listening to a taped recording. It is a guided journey into the mind's subconscious with visual aspects that can be used to alleviate stress or to create an outcome such as healing a health problem or assisting in accomplishing a goal. During such programs you may be instructed to use affirmations such as:

- I am healthy, vital, and strong.
- There is nothing in the world I cannot handle.
- I am completely and utterly safe.
- Every day in every way I am getting stronger.

While there is certainly no problem with using self-affirmation to get through stressful situations or to develop confidence, the problem with guided imagery is the belief that outcomes can be manipulated and altered through this process. Some guided-imagery programs actually suggest meeting a *being* in your mind to assist you. This is dangerous because it opens the door to spirits that are not of God. Sadly, countless Christians have jumped into this trend by creating their own version of guided imagery where they suggest *meeting* Jesus to act as a guide. This is problematic in that it creates a false belief that you are actually meeting and talking with Jesus in a mystical sense. There is no scriptural support that God chooses to communicate with us in this way.

Reiki

A practice that has become increasingly more popular in recent years, Reiki is a form of therapeutic touch. Unlike traditional massage, the premise of Reiki is based around a universal (chi) energy. A Reiki practitioner lays hands on the patient in order to impart some of this universal energy. Once again, without a scientific explanation, any results that do occur must be supernatural and if not of God, then who? The key to the success of Reiki healing is calling upon spirit guides to assist the practitioner in the healing process.

Today, thousands, if not millions of Reiki practitioners exist throughout the world, many claiming to be Christian. Type in the name Reiki on the Internet on Google and as of this writing it comes up over eight million times. Two years ago, that number was just one million. At that rate, in two more years the number will be over sixty million. Thousands of these web listings are on Christian web sites. But listen to this explanation from a renowned

Reiki master and decide for yourself if the term Christian Reiki practitioner is nothing but a blatant oxymoron:

> A Reiki attunement is an initiation into a sacred metaphysical order that has been present on earth for thousands of years.... By becoming part of this group, you will also be receiving help from the Reiki guides and other spiritual beings who are also working towards these goals.[11]

Paganism

Witchcraft/Wicca

Wicca is a relatively new pagan, religious practice, based upon nature-worship, and is, in actuality, none other than the age-old belief system of witchcraft. Little difference lies between the two. The word *Wicca* means to bend nature to your service. Many Eastern practices are incorporated into both witchcraft and wicca including the use of charms, candles, chanting and incense. Wicca is sometimes referred to as white witchcraft or witchcraft that is used for good. Wicca supporters believe there is a black witchcraft, a form that can be used for evil, which is different than Wicca. My question to these people is this: Isn't that like saying there are good drug dealers and bad drug dealers? In both types of witchcraft, the source of the power is the same, and it sure isn't from God.

Goddess/Gaia Worship

Gaia is the mythical Greek name for the Goddess of the Earth. The Gaia hypothesis is the belief that mother Earth is a single, self-regulating organism. Goddess worship is an empowering view for women by identifying God as feminine. Gaia worshippers, in general, consider Christianity their biggest enemy and oppose the view held by Christianity, Judaism and Islam of the masculine, patriarchal view of God, believing this diminishes the importance of women. Gaia has influenced much of today's environmental policy although it is an odd mixture of feminism and science, paganism and Eastern mysticism, all wrapped into one. Gaia practices include candles, incense, dancing, and chanting.

Crystal Healing

Crystal Healing is a technique performed by placing different stones on each of the seven chakras on the body, thus balancing energy and promoting healing. A crystal *healing* involves placing crystals of the appropriate color and energy at corresponding chakra points.

- Root chakra (base of the spine): Jasper (bloodstone), garnet, onyx, rubies
- Second chakra (abdomen): hematite, moonstone
- Third chakra (solar plexus): citrine, amber, topaz
- Fourth chakra (heart): rose quartz, Chinese Fluorite
- Fifth chakra (throat): aquamarine, turquoise
- Sixth chakra (third eye): sapphire, turquoise, amethyst
- Seventh chakra (crown): clear quartz or amethyst

Do crystals have power? Quartz can perhaps be used as a semi-conductor for electricity. However, it has no power of its own. The roots of this belief may be drawn from the use of talismans or amulets from centuries past. They are mere objects that occultists believe will evoke a spirit-driven power for healing.

To be perfectly blunt, crystals are rocks. Will placing rocks on your stomach take away pain? Can placing a rock on your forehead erase a headache? Many homes are filled with large quartz crystals sitting on their windowsills or coffee tables. People who own these believe the crystals will bring positive energy into the home. However, absolutely no scientific explanation for this belief exists; consequently if a certain energy or healing truly *is* obtained by using crystals, this energy must be a supernatural force. Yet, we must then ask ourselves, if it isn't God working through the crystals, where is the energy coming from?

Shamanism

A Shaman could be described as an Eastern version of a Native American medicine man. Shamanism is a belief in the existence of a world of spirits, mostly in animal form. Through a trance-like meditation that uses singing, dancing, and drumming, the entranced shaman can leave his or her body and travel in the spirit world. There, the Shaman works with spirit helpers to treat sickness and solve other problems afflicting clan members.

My friend Steve conducted classes in spiritual drumming. The drumming sessions would involve a group sitting in a circle, each member of the group holding a drum. The leader or Shaman would begin the beat, and the rest followed. Many would close their eyes and feel moved by the rhythm. The infectious power of the drums beating over and over would evoke a trance-like state. Many who participated said they had visions of Native Americans dancing around them. Some would hear spirits speaking to them during this time.

Labyrinths

A practice that has been around for thousands of years, labyrinths are now being introduced into Christian churches at an alarming rate. According to the International Labyrinth Society, "a labyrinth is a single path or unicursal tool for personal, psychological and spiritual transformation.... thought to enhance right brain activity." The labyrinth is a maze-like structure with actually only one path to the center, making it different from a typical maze that has several paths to choose from. Those using the labyrinths are encouraged to repeat a word or phrase while walking on the path so they may *center down*, thus reaching the *Divine within*. The assumption is that anyone can walk the labyrinth and find this Divinity. If such a notion were true (that God can be reached and connected to in this manner), then *connecting* to God through the Cross would not be necessary and the gospel would be made void. Many Christians do not realize what they are really partaking in when they walk the labyrinth. Nothing at all in Scripture supports its use. On the contrary, the premise of the labyrinth negates the message of Christ's sacrifice for our sins.

The New Age consists of many aspects and practices; but what is it that ties them all together? What would a person who does channeling have in common with Shakti Gawain? What would a motivational speaker have in common with a witch? It is what they believe about God.

"But who do you say that I am?"—Jesus

One wintery evening in 1997, I happened to switch on the television to an interview with Marianne Williamson, a popular New Age author. When asked about her beliefs regarding God, she said, "God is impersonal, but you can have a personal relationship with God."

At one time of my life, I would have nodded my head and thought her statement made perfect sense. But now I realize—it doesn't make any sense at all! *God is impersonal, but you can have a personal relationship with Him? This book you are holding in your hand is impersonal, but you can have a personal relationship with the book?* How can both be true?

In order to understand where New Agers are coming from, we must understand the heart and essence of the New Age movement—the beliefs and the reasoning (or lack thereof) behind it. Foremost, the **God* of the New Age is a convenient mixture of Monism and Pantheism—Monism, all is one, and Pantheism, all is *God*. *God* is a unifying field of energy, an impersonal force or unified consciousness. *God* is both good and bad, light and dark, male and female. Creation and creator are not distinguishable from one another.

This belief system borrows most of its ideas from Eastern religions, which is quite the opposite of religions that believe God is a *who* rather than an *it*. Buddhists, Hindus and New Agers believe *God* is impersonal. Jews, Muslims and Christians believe God is personal. An impersonal *God* can be described as being like an energy force or perhaps electricity. It has power, you can feel it and it is real. However, it cannot hear, feel, love, care or think.

A personal God has the ability to love, listen, see, feel, think

---

*While the word God is capitalized throughout this book, at times it is also italicized to distinguish between the biblical God and the New Age *God*.

and care. Marianne Williamson's view of God is fundamentally flawed. How can one have a personal relationship with an impersonal *God*? Her *God* doesn't know she is there. How can one have a relationship with a *God* that doesn't love? When I say most New Agers believe God is impersonal, that isn't completely accurate. They actually believe God is both personal and impersonal at the same time. While they sit in the lotus position in the morning meditating with the energy of the impersonal universal energy, they may spend the afternoon reading *Conversations With God*, by Neale Donald Walsch, a perfect example of believing in an impersonal *God* who communicates with us. But how can this impersonal universal energy speak?

Most New Agers who grew up in western civilization have been influenced by the Judeo-Christian view of God. This view is one that portrays God as a some*one* not a some*thing*. They relate to that view more than the Eastern impersonal portrayal of God, but they don't see the conflict. They do not see that the Eastern view of an impersonal *God* and the western view of a personal God are polar opposites and cannot be reconciled. They ignore the obvious dichotomy and essentially personalize an impersonal *God*.

Some might be puzzled as to why such an obvious contradiction would escape their notice. It is because they would never think that long or hard about it. They claim you cannot define God and that even to attempt to define God is to make Him small. They actually claim that all views about God are right and to assign any one identity to Him is arrogant and narrow-minded.

In my psychic-reading class, my instructor constantly reminded me that I thought too much. I tried to make sense of things that obviously didn't make sense. However, I, like many in the New Age, was so in love with the idea that I could control everything and become God-like that I turned off my brain and went along.

Take a look at these statements that paint an accurate picture of the mind set of which I speak:

Kneel to your own self. Honor and worship your
own being. God dwells within you as You.
—**Swami Muktananda**, a Hindu mystic

Remember, but for the grace of God, we would not be
God.—**Paul Williams**, *Das Energi*

God lies within, and therefore, we are each part of God.
Since there is no separateness, we are each Godlike, and
God is in each of us. We are literally made up of God
energy; therefore, we can create whatever we want in life
because we are each co-creating with the energy of God—
the energy that makes the universe itself.—**Shirley
MacLaine**, *Going Within*

In a sense there is no such thing as God, God does not
exist. And in another sense, there is nothing else but God,
only God exists.... This microphone is God. This table
is God. All is God. And because all is God, there is no
God... God is everything that you have ever known or
could ever know and everything beyond your level of
knowing.[12]—**Benjamin Crème**

This the being/embodiment relationship, as
exemplified primarily in the Eastern religions and
philosophies.... This relationship simply affirms that
all life is one, that I am one with God and can embody
Divinity.... God and I do not just communicate; we
commune and are one. There is no separation except
failure to recognize that there is no separation.—**David
Spangler**, *Revelation*

I know that I exist, therefore I AM. I know that the God
source exists. Therefore IT IS. Since I am part of that force,
then I AM that I AM.[13]—**Shirley MacLaine**

I was six when I saw that everything was God ... My sister
was only a very tiny child then, and she was drinking her

milk, and all of a sudden I saw that *she* was God and the *milk* was God. I mean, all that she was doing was pouring God into God.[14]—**J.D. Salinger**

We already know everything. The knowingness of our divinity is the highest intelligence. And to be what we already know is the free will. Free will is simply the enactment of the realization that you are God, a realization that you are divine.[15]—**Shirley MacLaine**

As you finish reading this chapter you may be saying to yourself, "Well, fine and dandy—Brian has convinced us that New Age practices and the belief system behind them are certainly not scriptural and should not be played around with, but what do they have to do with me? I'm not playing with Ouija boards and trying to contact spirit guides." But before you dismiss my words too quickly, there is more to this story. A deception lies in our midst, and when the outer layers are stripped away, what lies beneath is a shocking discovery of something that has the potential of destroying the very essence and life of a Christianity that worships and adores Jesus Christ alone.

Truth and Lies

I can disagree with doctrines and dogmas, and still celebrate them. I go to the synagogue. I study Hinduism. [Religion is] about realizing that all paths lead to God in the end, and that everybody decided ... to sort of segregate and say, 'No, these are my rules. No, I believe that God came from here. No, I believe that Jesus is not the Son of God. No, I believe in this, and I believe in that.' And the thing is ... they're all the same.—Madonna, July 27, 1999, Sixty Minutes

If New Agers and postmodernists have one common unifying thread that weaves them together, it is their belief that all paths lead to God. No right answer, no wrong answer. Whatever you choose to believe about God is true. And any and all of those beliefs lead to the same place ... right into the arms of an all-embracing *God*.

Hey Man, That's Your Truth.

In an attempt to share the gospel of Christ with New Agers, I have heard one reply, over and over, "Well, that's your truth, Brian. I have a different one." What a preposterous notion! How is this even possible! The presupposition of the New Ager is that you have your own truth. They are mixing up the word truth with opinion. You can certainly have your own opinion but a different truth? You cannot own the truth. Something either is or it isn't true. The holocaust either happened or it didn't. I do not get to *choose* whether it happened or not. JFK was either shot or he wasn't.

It either happened or it did not; my opinion is completely irrelevant. I wish very much that the Vikings would have won the Super Bowl, but do I have a choice whether it happened or not? I prefer it if slavery had never occurred in our country, but do I get to choose that it did not happen simply because I don't like that it happened? Why should it be any different when choosing the truth about God? The most important questions every human being needs to have answered are: Is there a God? What is the truth about God? Who is God?

If I asked a simple question such as, what is 2 + 2, the answer of course is obvious. However, what if you met a group of people who came from a sheltered society on a desert island who believed that 2 + 2 equaled 5—a sum their fathers believed, their grandfathers believed, and all their ancestors believed. Are they correct because it is what they have believed for as long as they can remember? New Age and postmodern thinking says we shouldn't make judgments, and if it is someone else's truth, we should respect it; to accommodate their feelings, we should declare that $2+2= 4 \frac{1}{2}$.

Did O. J. Simpson kill his wife or not? Some believe he was set up and that he was indeed innocent. Others feel strongly that he was guilty. No matter what side you take, we can agree upon one thing—the answer isn't both. He is either guilty of the crime, or he isn't.

New Age writer, Neale Donald Walsch, describes truth in his book, *Communion With God*, as something that is always changing:

> Truth is nothing more than a word meaning "what is right now." However, since conditions are always changing, changing conditions create changing truth.[1]

What is truth to the postmodernist? For the most radical of postmodernists there is no *objective* reality outside of ourselves that we can call true. Consequently, objective reality is swallowed up into *subjective* thinking where we, the thinkers, become the arbitrators of what is true. Truth then becomes a matter of social negotiations and the majority consensus rather than anything we can glean from observation.

In other words, truth is what *we* tell you it is. We, the intelligentsia, we the postmodernists, we, who are smarter than you—we know the truth! The New Agers see truth as subjective because the postmodernist philosophy permeates their thinking. The postmodernist does not believe in a God who is an authority above man deciding the confines of good and evil. One man's truth cannot be more right than another man's truth. So how can one decide what is true at all?

Who can decide? If man is the ultimate arbiter of truth, then truth is whatever man determines it to be. Therefore, evil is simply an opinion. The unfortunate outcome is that evil, when left unchecked, grows unabated. By the time the postmodernist realizes his world has changed for the worse because of his moral relativist position, it is too late. He becomes a victim of the evil he didn't believe existed.

Is God Personal?

How can God be both impersonal and personal all at the same time? How can both ideas be true? A personal God is one who thinks—an impersonal God does not. One has personage; the other is like a force or energy. New Agers will say that God could choose to be a potted plant for a day also. However, in order to do so, He would have to choose to become a potted plant. If He is choosing, then He is thinking. If He is thinking, then He is a personal God. New Age reasoning attempts to personalize an impersonal God. But herein lies the problem—if a right answer exists about God, then there must also be a wrong answer. So how can these two opposing ideas about God—personal and impersonal—both be true? Such a contradiction should create conflict in the mind of someone seeking truth and force him to search elsewhere.

Logic or Feelings?

One day I asked a friend of mine:

> What if your brother decided to move to California by himself? Several months pass, and you have not heard from him. One night he calls to tell you goodbye. He has found a group of people that he has connected with and now knows the truth about God. He has joined the remnants of the Heaven's Gate group.

The Heaven's Gate Cult made the news on March 26, 1997 when Marshall Applewhite and his followers downed vodka, phenobarbital and pudding, convinced that by shedding their containers [their bodies] they would hitch a ride to paradise aboard a spaceship trailing the Hale-Bopp comet.[2] They saw the appearance of the Hale-Bopp comet as a marker in time. Applewhite convinced all of them that they must commit suicide in order to meet their cosmic spaceship.

Your brother tells you he has discovered there is still time to catch the spaceship, and he intends to take a phenobarbital and vodka tonic tonight and head out. He is going to commit suicide. Here is your dilemma: do you support him because everything is truth or do you stop him because you know that the Heavens Gate cult was wrong?

My friend hesitated, realizing the implications of the story. With some hesitance, she answered, "I would try to talk him out of it. Those guys are all nuts!"

Through this story, my friend realized that not everything believed is truth. If there is a wrong answer, then there must be a right answer. The reason she was willing to acquiesce and acknowledge my point was that I approached her through her *feelings*. The cost of being "correct" would have meant the loss of her brother. The New Age is filled with lovely platitudes by which to live life. However, when push comes to shove, these principles and premises will be abandoned with a quick dash to Judeo-Christian values.

And What About Jesus?

I s the story about Jesus true? If so, we know who God is. Jesus Christ claimed to be God, and in saying this, He had to be either speaking the truth, or He was a liar. If He was speaking the truth, all other beliefs about God would, of course, be wrong. If we know He is God, all other thoughts, ideas and religions are now considered null and void. Right?

Do I get to choose that His life, death and resurrection didn't happen? No, but I can choose to ignore that it happened. Many people choose to say the story of Jesus is not true because they do not want it to be true. Seldom has someone studied the evidence, and declared it a legend. Most people make up their minds without even giving it a second thought.

The New Ager states that the Bible was written by men with an agenda. He will say the Bible is full of mistakes because men will interpret events in their own way, and it could never be trusted to be accurate. But the Bible says, "knowing this first, that no prophecy of Scripture is of any private interpretation, for prophecy never came by the will of man, but holy men of God spoke as they were moved by the Holy Spirit" (II Peter 1: 20, 21).

If I were a scientist who lived 500 years ago and fervently believed the earth was flat, could I choose to ignore the trip of Ferdinand Magellan? I could, but am I being a real scientist, one who seeks evidence to prove a theory? Am I being honest and objective? Maybe it is my pride that prevents me from looking at the evidence. If I look at the evidence honestly and with an open mind, am I afraid it will prove me wrong? If the evidence is there to prove that the story of Jesus is true, then everything I once thought about God will have to be reconsidered. Choices, behavior, and even life itself will have to be reexamined. No wonder there is a rejection of Christianity. To accept Christianity means to accept the fact that mankind is sinful and needs a Savior.

A Holy God and Sinners

As I shared earlier, the evidence, which supports the authenticity of the Bible and Jesus Christ, is extremely compelling. However, will everyone who views that evidence become a Christian? No. "But the natural man does not receive the things of the Spirit of God, for they are foolishness to him; nor can he know them, because they are spiritually discerned" (I Corinthians 2:14).

Why is it that after clearly seeing evidence of Jesus and the Bible so many still turn away? Could it be the enticements of the world are too great? Is it the fear of having to leave seductive and destructive behaviors behind that keep many from walking down the road of truth? "Because narrow is the gate and difficult is the way which leads to life, and there are few who find it" (Matthew 7:14).

Prior to becoming a Christian, I could not fathom the concept of living pure and righteously. I knew I would fail, so why even try? What I did not know was that God has promised to send a counselor, the Holy Spirit, to be my guide and my strength: "And I will pray the Father, and He will give you another Helper, that He may abide with you forever" (John 14:16).

God has given us a wonderful gift, the Holy Spirit, to assist us in resisting temptation. Why did He do that? Because He knew we humans were weak—our very nature is weak and sinful. It is more in our nature to sin than to do what is right. It is because of this that the heavenly Father sent His Son to die. Fortunately for us, He died for the sins of the past, the present and yes, for the future too. Does this make us immune from all sin once we become Christians? Absolutely not ... in fact, the apostle Paul said the very things he tries not to do, he ends up doing and the things he should be doing, he can't seem to do (Romans 7). But because of God's grace, once we confess our sins to Him, He is quick to forgive us our sins. The Bible says if we resist the devil, he will flee from us. But we must resist, fully realizing that when we choose not to and willingly go the way of sin, there are consequences.

As a former New Ager, I never knew what was truly right or wrong because it was always up to me. Having been given the gift of the Holy Spirit, I now see that true guidance is found in God's written Word. The Bible reveals God's will, and for the Christian, the Holy Spirit gives one the power, desire, and motivation to do God's will. I am never alone and void of God's guidance.

The Nature of Demons

> Therefore it is no great thing if [Satan's] ministers also transform themselves into ministers of righteousness. (II Corinthians 11:15)

When I performed psychic readings for people, they enjoyed it and felt it really helped them. In many instances the information I shared with them turned out to be accurate. But if I am right when I say the source of these readings was evil and actually given by demons, why would demons do something to help people?

After a reading, many of my clients would return asking about other concerns in their lives. If I was right on some things then it would stand to reason in their minds that I would be correct on the other dilemmas of life that confront them. The purpose for all demons is only one thing—to keep as many people as possible from seeking Jesus Christ.

By performing readings, I was giving these demons a big helping hand—those who came to me became dependent on my readings, and it certainly kept them from seeking the Lord. And of course, what they heard from the demons through me was exactly what they wanted to hear. God, on the other hand, probably would have been telling them how to straighten out their lives.

It surprised me that even when I was wrong about something, many people still returned to me searching for answers. Often they struggled with the moral issues of their desires and hoped for some affirmation. One young man in his early twenties came to me for a reading and asked me about a woman he desired, wanting to know if he should pursue the relationship. My guides told me without hesitation that he should. It was many years later that I discovered he was married and the women he wanted was not his wife. He pursued the relationship and got her pregnant. His wife left him, and later the other woman broke off the relationship. He ended up alone, losing both women and causing a lot of heartbreak. Would God have given him the same advice? My spirit guides gave him the answer he wanted to hear. They also gave him the answer that would destroy his marriage. Demons destroy. That is their nature. They did it in the Garden of Eden with Adam and Eve, and they are still doing it today. And yet they disguise themselves, as Scripture says, as workers of good.

Looking back at my own relationship with Hailey, I can see

the ugliness of my behavior towards her. As I described, we were vicious to each other. I believe my *helpful* spirit guides were instrumental in breaking up my marriage. While I take responsibility for my failure in the marriage, I now recognize my behavior and anger were fueled by the constant demonic influences in my life. At the time, I saw them as helpers. I thought my spirit guides were there to comfort and guide me. Why would they seek to destroy my relationship with Hailey?

It reminds me of the story of the snake and the mouse: One day after a heavy rainstorm a large stream formed, separating a mouse from his home. The stream was too wide and deep for him to cross. As he sat on the stream's edge a snake crawled up next to him. The mouse screamed and said, "Please don't eat me!"

The snake answered back, "I have no intention of eating you. But why are you waiting at the stream's edge?"

"I need to get across to the other side to my home, but the stream is too wide and too deep for me to cross," replied the little mouse.

Smiling, the snake said, "I will help you. Just climb on my back, and I will take you across."

The mouse hesitated and said, "No. As soon as you get to the other side you will eat me."

"I assure you, I will do no such thing," replied the snake. Finally the mouse succumbed, climbed on the snake's back, and off they swam to the other side of the lake. As the mouse got off his back, the snake wrapped himself around him holding him tight.

"You said you wouldn't eat me!" the mouse screamed.

The snake replied, "*I am a snake—this is what I do.*"

Demons cannot help but be who they are. They are destroyers. They pitted my wife and me against each other and fueled the fire of anger and mistrust. With all the helpful information they shared with me, they never once told me I was going to lose my wife, my car, and my house. I was, to put it plainly, possessed by demons—not a crazed prisoner but a willing possession. The tactic of demons is to speak through willing subjects as they proclaim their blasphemies through channelers to lead people down the road to destruction.

After my conversion, I received a call from a friend who was still channeling. She asked, "Why did you become a Christian?"

I chose my words carefully and said, "I got tired of being a receptacle." There was a long pause. She knew what I meant. Unfortunately, it wasn't enough to convince her to leave the channeling behind. The money and notoriety she achieved was too hard to let go of.

I ran into her a few years later and was shocked at how bedraggled and aged she looked. After all the years she spent channeling, it had done her nothing but harm. When someone has demons trampling in and out of his or her soul day after day, year after year, eventually all life is sucked right out.

Speaking to the Dead

> And when they say to you, "Seek those who are mediums and wizards, who whisper and mutter," should not a people seek their God? Should they seek the dead on behalf of the living? (Isaiah 8: 19, 20)

On April 3, 1998, medium James Van Praagh appeared on ABC's news magazine 20/20. On the show the producers had selected people at random to be *read* by James who claims to have the ability to speak to the dead.

The host brought in two women whom Van Praagh had never met before. While he did not seem to connect at all with the first woman, the second was a different story. He told her he was speaking to her dead father:

> **Van Praagh:** Your father keeps on talking about shining the shoes, making sure his shoes are shined?
> **Woman:** [W]hen I was little, that was my job. When I was a little tiny kid, I would shine his shoes.

The woman then asked Van Praagh if her father was all right. James responded, "He says he will give you a quarter." The woman's face turned to shock.

"That's my father," the woman exclaimed. "After I would shine his shoes he would give me a quarter. As the years passed it became a private joke between us that when things were good he would say, 'I will give you a quarter.'"[3]

How did Van Praagh know such a thing? How did he get it right? Was it a scam? I can tell you from first-hand experience, it was no scam.

Of course there are fraudulent psychics who try to embellish their readings. It's the authentic ones I wish to discuss though.

James Van Praagh and a man named John Edward are two of the most prominent mediums in today's pop culture. Van Praagh has written four books, *Talking to Heaven, Reaching to Heaven, Healing Grief,* and *Heaven and Earth.*

John Edward has also written several books but is most famous for his show *Crossing Over* airing on the Sci-Fi Channel. I watched John Edward on Larry King Live one evening as he took calls from across America. One call got my attention. He told the woman caller that he was in contact with her dead father. She was concerned about him and the issues in her own life after he had passed away. Edward asked the woman if she kept a gun in her bed. When she acknowledged that she did, Edward told her the message from her father was, "You don't need to do that anymore. You will be safe without it."

How are these men able to give these accurate answers? They of course would defend the notion that they are indeed talking to the dead. Without question, I used to believe this myself. Now I know the truth. It is not the dead they are talking to but rather demons, demons who have knowledge of the dead.

Why is it that the most important information any live person would want to hear from a dead person is never communicated?: What is the truth about Heaven, Hell, or God? If I were dead and had a chance to speak with a living relative, the first thing I would tell them is *Jesus is Lord! Don't follow any other God! If you do, you will go to Hell!* But such things are never communicated when a medium is *speaking to the dead.* The information shared has some accuracy because demons have knowledge of the deceased—not all knowledge but just enough to sound convincing.

If the dead could truly speak to us, they would want to warn us of the impending judgment and the existence of Heaven and Hell. In the last chapter, I alluded to Jesus' parable of the rich man and Lazarus and what it had to say about reincarnation. Now, let's look in more depth at the actual text and see what Jesus has to say regarding communication with the dead. After reading this I think you will have to conclude as I did that mediums are not talking to the dead at all but rather demons:

> There was a certain rich man who was clothed in purple and fine linen and fared sumptuously every day. But there was a certain beggar named Lazarus, full of sores, who was laid at his gate, desiring to be fed with the crumbs which fell from the rich man's table. Moreover the dogs came and licked his sores.

> So it was that the beggar died, and was carried by the angels to Abraham's bosom. The rich man also died and was buried. And being in torments in Hades, he lifted up his eyes and saw Abraham afar off, and Lazarus in his bosom.

> Then he cried and said, "Father Abraham, have mercy on me, and send Lazarus that he may dip the tip of his finger in water and cool my tongue; for I am tormented in this flame." But Abraham said, "Son, remember that in your lifetime you received your good things, and likewise Lazarus evil things; but now he is comforted and you are tormented. And besides all this, between us and you there is a great gulf fixed, so that those who want to pass from here to you cannot, nor can those from there pass to us."

> Then he said, "I beg you therefore, father, that you would send him to my father's house, for I have five brothers, that he may testify to them, lest they also come to this place of torment." Abraham said to him, "They have Moses and the prophets; let them hear them." And he said, "No, father Abraham; but if one

goes to them from the dead, they will repent." But he said to him, "If they do not hear Moses and the prophets, neither will they be persuaded though one rise from the dead." (Luke 16:19-31)

In the parable, the rich man is not able to speak to his brothers nor does God allow Lazarus, who is in Heaven, to speak either. Why is this? Why does God not allow communication between the living and the dead? According to this parable, Abraham explains that they have the testimony of God's laws and His prophets (the Word of God) that clearly describes everything they need to know. A sign coming from a dead person would not compel their faith anyway. Even when Jesus brought back a person named Lazarus from the dead, it didn't result in Israel coming to faith, nor did Jesus' resurrection from the dead convince the religious leaders of the day that He is Lord.

God prevents the dead from speaking to us for the same reason. He has given us all we need to know to gain entrance to Heaven through Jesus Christ and the Bible. He does not need a dead person to convince us that He is the way, the truth, and the life.

Truth Within?

Many today attempt to find truth but only accept the one that does not interfere with the way they wish to live. The dogma of Christianity is too restrictive to accept. Therefore, they search for a *truth* that is comfortable and appealing.

Are there multiple truths? Certainly there are multiple opinions, but opinion and truth are not the same thing. If there is no absolute truth then the New Ager is constantly trying to find solid ground to stand upon. The shifting sands of truth of postmodernism only offer confusion. One day certain behaviors are wrong, the next day they are right. Without knowing what is true and what is false, the only avenues of information chosen are those that do not include Christ, and present-day soothsayers, mediums, psychics, and self-help gurus are at the service of all who cry out for answers:

> Debbie Ford, ... a faculty member at ... Deepak
> Chopra Center for Wellbeing [and author of *The Dark
> Side of the Light Chasers*] reveals the frustration brewing
> among her devotees: "In my seminars I often work
> with people who have invested years of therapy,
> transformational seminars, breath work, and other
> healing modalities. They ask the same questions: 'when
> will it end? When will I be done? How much more
> work must I do on the issues that come up over and
> over again?'"[4]

The answer? Without Christ, it will never end.

Once I became a Christian, I found I no longer needed to divine my future. Because of Christ, I know who I am, who the Father is, and where my future lies. My constant journey from one New Age seminar to the next, from one guru to the next, from one spiritual book of *truth* to the next and my never being able to find rest or satisfaction all came to a screeching halt. The Truth of all life stood before me like an immovable pillar and changed my life forever.

While Christians need to be telling a lost world about this truth, the philosophies and beliefs of Satan swirl around in the minds and hearts of the unbelieving. In a world that says we all have *divinity* and *truth* within, is it not the responsibility of every born-again believer to stand firmly and courageously for the message of the Cross, which alone can save a soul and unite it to God?

All Paths Lead to God?

[E]very morning.... I watch the sun come up and I
center myself and try to touch the God light that I
believe is in all of us.... I just call it centering up.... If
there happens to be a day when I don't do it, I find
myself loose, misdirected.[1]—Oprah Winfrey

Oprah Winfrey is, by far, the most influential person when it
comes to promoting books. Unfortunately, her selections of
books are generally New Age. I had at one time believed Oprah to
be a Christian. Often she has spoken about her upbringing, always
mentioning how the church shaped her life. However, the statements
she makes on her shows and in more current interviews clearly ex-
pose her New Age views: "One of the biggest mistakes humans
make is to believe there is only one way. There are many diverse
paths leading to what you call God."[2]

I believe Oprah is well-intentioned, and I think everyone agrees
she is one of the most generous and well thought of people in America.
However, that doesn't make her right. Sincere—yes; right—no.

During one of her shows that focused on reincarnation, the Christian Bible was attacked and grossly misinterpreted. On that show, Oprah
stated, "As I study the New Age movement, it all seems to say exactly
what the Bible has said for years, but many of us were brought up
with a restricted, limited understanding of what the Bible said."

Donald Curtis, a Unity minister and trance channeler and a guest
on that show, responded to Oprah by saying, "No one really knows

what the filter of translation [has done] down through the ages, what the Bible really said."

Marilyn Ferguson, another New Age leader, chimed in: "When you start taking a scholarly look at when the translations occurred you realize that many important ideas got lost along the way." Curtis heartily agreed, adding:

> [T]hey threw out most of it in 325 A.D. anyway at the Council of Nicea. We don't really know what was there. The Emperor, whatever his name was, sat down in counsel and said, 'this is in and this is out.' They threw out reincarnation at this time.[3]

Anyone with any knowledge of history knows this is not true. Arius, a leader of the Baucalis Church, came into conflict with his bishop, Alexander. Sometime around 318, Arius openly challenged teachers in Alexandria by asserting that the Word (Logos) who became flesh in Jesus Christ (John 1:14) was not the true God and that He had an entirely different nature, neither eternal nor omnipotent. Bishop Alexander, however, would have none of it. He called a synod at Alexandria about 320, and the assembled churchmen condemned Arius' teaching and excommunicated the pastor.

The Emperor, Constantine, recognized that the explosive issue had to be diffused. So, in 325, he called for the council of bishops to meet in Nicea. The assembly denounced Arius' idea, calling it blasphemy.[4] From that meeting the Nicene Creed emerged.

The meeting in Nicea was not about tossing out the concept of reincarnation; it was about protecting the truth about Christ's deity. But how would the average viewer of Oprah's show know that?

When Oprah invited Betty Eadie, author of *Embraced by the Light*, Ms. Eadie shared her story of her near death experience. She claimed that in 1973 she was *dead* for several hours and during that time, she said her spirit was transported to Heaven. While there, she was allegedly embraced by Jesus Christ and given a tour of Heaven. "When Eadie told Oprah that the 'Jesus' she met showed her that "all religions lead to God," Winfrey immediately responded, 'That's what I believe.'"[5]

Marianne and A Course in Miracles

When Marianne Williamson appeared on Oprah's show in 1992 promoting her book, *A Return to Love: Reflections on the Principles of a Course in Miracles*, she sold out the 70,000-copy first printing in one day.

Marianne's *reflections* were based upon a book called *A Course in Miracles* written by Helen Schucman, a professor of Medical Psychology at Columbia University who took "dictation" from an "inner voice" that she recognized as Jesus. In the years since, *A Course in Miracles* has resulted in an international spiritual movement expressive in two foundations: Inner Peace, an administrative and publishing arm, and the Foundation for *A Course in Miracles*, a teaching arm which is in more than 2000 study groups in this country alone, at least 50 newsletters, and 25 teaching centers.[6]

Helen's *Jesus* told her the Bible needed correction. It took from 1965 to 1972 to complete all *Jesus* had to say. I guess *Jesus* had a lot to correct. Her *Jesus* began by saying, "This is a course in miracles, please take notes."

These are some of the corrections that *Jesus* had to make to the Bible:

God—

- God is your identity, you will be like God.
- God's Name is holy, but no holier than yours.
- To call upon His Name is but to call upon your own.
- God Himself is incomplete without me.
- God and man are not separated. The writings teach that God and His creation are one.
- If you are part of one you must be part of the other, because they are one. The Holy Trinity is holy because it is One. If you exclude yourself from this union, you perceive the Holy Trinity as separated.
- There is no separation of God and His creation.
- The Kingdom of Heaven is the dwelling place of the Son of God, who left not his Father and dwells not apart from Him. Heaven is not a place nor condition. It is merely the awareness of perfect

oneness, and the knowledge that there is nothing else; nothing outside this oneness, and nothing else within. [7]

Salvation—

- We do not need a savior. We are the source of our own salvation.
- My salvation comes from me. Nothing outside of me can hold me back. Within me is the world's salvation and my own.
- He will teach you how to see yourself without condemnation, by learning how to look on everything without it. Condemnation will then not be real to you, and all your errors will be forgiven.

Sin—

- There is no sin, it is all an illusion.
- And therefore all your sins have been forgiven because they carried no effects at all. And so they were but dreams.
- Do not make the pathetic error of "clinging to the old rugged Cross." The only message of the crucifixion is that you can overcome the Cross. Until then you are free to crucify yourself as often as you choose. This is not the Gospel I intended to offer you. [8]

Helen's *Jesus* did not intend to give us the Gospel we have now. He meant to give us the pantheistic (everything is God) bible. He meant to give us the moral relativist bible. He meant to give us the bible which is more aligned with Hinduism than anything else.

I am amazed at how many people believe and adhere to *A Course in Miracles*. I overheard a woman on a plane in the seat across from me telling her friend she believed every word in it. Many intelligent people take the word of one woman who says she heard voices in her head over the time-tested authenticity of the Bible.

Worse yet, countless churches in America use this book in place of Bible study. Why would they do such a thing? According to one pastor, "My congregation likes it." I'm sure they do—it absolves them from sin without repentance.

The reason this book plays well for many baby boomers who

left the church when they were kids and are now starting to come back is because it *sounds* like Christianity. The language of the book is very Christian. Since they have little biblical knowledge they are easily duped. For the uninformed, it is the perfect book, combining the familiarity of Christianity with moral relativism and pantheism. Many people today want the comfort the church can give without all the inconvenient repentance part—and certainly not the part that says there is only one way to God.

Marianne Williamson, who has fashioned herself after Helen Schucman and her Course in Miracles attempts to personalize an impersonal God who is an energy or force she calls love:

> The love in one of us is the love in all of us. There's actually no place where God stops and you start, and no place where you stop and I start. Love is energy, an infinite continuum.[9]

In this statement, God is impersonal. However, in other parts of the book she prays to *him* and states that *he* guides our thoughts and feelings. Again she refers to God as impersonal and then back to personal. She can't seem to make up her mind. This idea is not uncommon with the New Ager. He may pray to a God whom he sees in his mind, who cares about him in the morning, and then whom he later tries to connect to as a God-like energy by aligning his chakras in the afternoon. At no time does it occur to him that he is living in complete spiritual contradiction.

One of the themes of the New Age is the reference to Jesus and Christ as being separate from each other. Jesus was one who embodied the *Christ consciousness*, the attitude of complete love and forgiveness, better than anyone else. The Christ consciousness is a goal or an indwelling spirit to be obtained—not a separate God to be worshipped.

New Age writer David Spangler wrote a book titled *Reflections on the Christ*, in which he states that Jesus was an ordinary (though quite spiritual) human being who became a vehicle through which *the Christ* manifested himself for a short period of three years.

After this time, at the crucifixion, the Christ departed from the body of Jesus, having fully accomplished his mission:

> The Christ ... is a mighty spirit being (or force) who utilized the body of Jesus in order to become a potent evolutionary influence in man's development on Earth. The Christ needed the body of Jesus in order to make the transfer from his own realm (that is, the spiritual realm) to the realm of Jesus (that is, the realm of matter and form).[10]

Marianne believes this same concept:

> Jesus ... was one who perfectly embodied the Christ (love) essence and hence is a perfect model for the rest of us. The special thing about Jesus is that he was a perfect vehicle for the "Christ." But we can do just as he did. Jesus fully "accepted" Christ, and so can we!
>
> The concept of a divine, or "Christ" mind, is the idea that, at our core, we are not just identical, but actually the same being. "There is only one begotten Son" doesn't mean that someone else was it, and we're not. It means we're all it.... Christ refers to the common thread of divine love that is the core and essence of every human mind.[11]

This of course contradicts the Bible: "And the Word became flesh and dwelt among us, and we beheld His glory, the glory as of the only begotten of the Father, full of grace and truth" (John 1:14).

The underlying theme of Marianne Williamson's belief system goes back to the Bible when Lucifer said we can become like God. In an interview with *In Touch* magazine, Marianne stated:

> Because the world as it is perceived by most people, is a world of finite resources.... Jesus was able to do the miracles of the loaves and the fishes because he realized that he was not a being of this world. When we realize

that we are not beings of this world, we are freed from being at the effects of those laws.[12]

Marianne believes we have unlimited power available to us or she would not have written a book about it. However, she has yet to duplicate the miracle Jesus performed with the loaves and fishes. Granted, she has sold thousands of books and made a lot of money, proving that a great source of wealth can be gained by writing about this subject. Selling 70,000 books after one appearance on Oprah might be considered a miracle.

The poor audience on Oprah's show ponies up hard-earned money to buy books like this, hoping they too can enjoy the benefits that Marianne promises. Is Marianne right? Or has she followed the philosophy of another *great* mind to produce her *miracle*— P.T. Barnum. To paraphrase Barnum's most notable quote, there is an infinite source of fools born everyday looking for God, wealth, and happiness in all the wrong places.

Marianne and others like her stand ready at the till.

Conversations with Whom?

Neale Donald Walsch, who wrote *Conversations With God*, is considered one of the most prominent people in today's New Age spirituality. His book took shape when Walsch became frustrated with his life after four failed marriages, and he decided to write a letter to God. He picked up a yellow legal pad and began to pour out his frustrations. He wrote:

> *What have I done to deserve a life of such continuing struggle?* To my surprise, as I scribbled out the last of my bitter, unanswerable questions and prepared to toss my pen aside, my hand remained poised over the paper, as if held there by some invisible force. Abruptly, the pen began *moving on its own.* I had no idea what I was about to write, but an idea seemed to be coming, so I decided to flow with it. Out came…

Do you really want answers to all these questions, or are you just venting?[13]

Thus begins Walsch's conversations with *God*, and *we* get to read what *God* says.

Conversations With God has been extremely popular, and Walsch has written several follow-up books along the same line: *Conversations With God Book 2, Conversations With God Book 3, Communion With God, Questions and Answers on Conversations With God* and of course, not to leave out a book for our youth, *Conversations With God for Teens.*

Let's take a look at some of these *conversations* Neale has had with *God*. In this particular conversation, Neale is discussing right from wrong with *God*:

> **Walsch:** But those who have taught me all about the rights and wrongs, the dos and don'ts, the shoulds and shouldn'ts, told me all those rules were laid down by *You*—by *God.*
>
> **God:** Then those who taught you were wrong. I have never set down a "right" or "wrong," a "do" or a "don't." To do so would be to strip you completely of your greatest gift—the opportunity to do as you please, and experience the results of that.... To say something—a thought, a word, an action—is "wrong" would be as much as to tell you not to do it.... To prohibit you would be to restrict you. To restrict you would be to deny the reality of Who You Really Are.[14]

This kind of talk is sweet music to the moral relativist who loves to hear and believe people are *Divine* and are thus God. Walsch later asks *God* about good and evil only to get the following response:

> **God:** Evil is that which you *call* evil. Yet even that I love, for it is only through that which you call evil that you can know good; only through that which you call the work of the devil that you can know and do the work of God. I do

not love hot more than I do cold, high more than low, left more than right. It is *all relative*. It is all part of *what is*.

I do not love "good" more than I love "bad." Hitler went to heaven. When you understand this, you will understand God.[15]

Let's examine what *God* is saying. *God's* plan is to allow you to do as you please even if it harms others. One of the few behaviors left in our society that makes even New Agers recoil is pedophilia, so let's use that as the example. Is it therefore God's plan to allow us to harm children to teach us to know what good is? God doesn't love the *good* of protecting children from a pedophile more than the *bad* of allowing it to happen? Neale's *God* is sick.

And what was that he said about Hitler? He's going to Heaven too? Why does Walsch's *God* write this? Is it to convince us Hell or punishment do not exist—that we can do no wrong in the eyes of God? We can do anything we want without consequences or guilt, in which case we do not need to ask for forgiveness and therefore certainly have no need for the Cross of Jesus Christ. This is the freedom man has longed for—to be autonomous, to be God. The declaration in Walsch's first book that Hitler too will go to Heaven must have caused a stir, even for New Agers, for in his second book, he clarifies:

> **God**: Hitler went to heaven for these reasons: There is no hell, so there is no place else for him to go. His actions were what you call mistakes—the actions of an unevolved being—and mistakes are not punishable by condemnation, but dealt with by providing the chance for correction, for evolution. The mistakes Hitler made did no harm or damage to those whose deaths he caused. Those souls were released from their earthly bondage, like butterflies emerging from a cocoon.[16]

He did no harm or damage by the deaths he caused? The families of the millions he killed never wept a tear? The children of parents who died in Auschwitz never experienced loss? The wives that survived their husbands' murders and torture never experienced pain?

In this next exchange *God* describes the way in which to know what truth is and how to make all of life's decisions:

> **God:** You cannot know God until you've stopped telling yourself that you *already* know God. You cannot hear God until you stop thinking that you've already heard God. I cannot tell you my Truth until you stop telling Me yours.
>
> **Walsch:** But my truth about God comes from *You.*
>
> **God:** Who said so?
>
> **Walsch:** Leaders. Ministers. Rabbis. Priests. Books. The *Bible,* for heaven's sake!
>
> **God:** Those are not authoritative sources.
>
> **Walsch:** They *aren't?*
>
> **God:** No.
>
> **Walsch:** Then what *is?*
>
> **God:** Listen to your *feelings.* Listen to your Highest Thoughts. Listen to your experience. Whenever any one of these differ from what you have been told by your teachers, or read in your books, forget the words. *Words* are the least reliable purveyor of Truth.[17]

Whenever you are told something different by teachers or what you have read in books, ignore them and do as you wish. I feel it, therefore it is right. I wonder if Eric Harris and Dylan Klebold who committed the murders at Columbine High School took this same type of advice.

It would seem that Walsch's *God* allows you to do anything you please, but no, wait a minute:

> **God:** If you ever lit a cigarette in your life—much less smoked a pack a day for 20 years as you have—you have very little will to live. You don't care what you do to your body.
>
> **Walsch:** But I *stopped* smoking over 10 years ago!
>
> **God:** Only after 20 years of grueling physical punishment. And if you've ever taken alcohol into your body, you have very little will to live.

> **Walsch:** I drink very moderately.
> **God:** The body was not meant to intake alcohol. It
> impairs the mind.[18]

Now all of a sudden *God* is upset with a choice. It is okay for
Hitler to kill millions of people but not okay for Neale Donald
Walsch to smoke or drink?

> **Walsch:** But *Jesus* took alcohol! He went to the
> wedding and turned water into wine!
> **God:** So who said Jesus was perfect?[19]

It seems that *God* is now contradicting Himself. If he was the
true God, wouldn't you expect him to be consistent? Unchanging?
He allows you to do what you please, but if you drink or smoke,
that is … wrong? I thought no rights or wrongs existed!

Is Walsch's *God* a God of love? If you can remember back to
the time when you were a teenager and your parents had control
over you, I'm sure there were times when you wished they didn't.
If only they would allow you to do as you please.

Isn't one of the expressions of love a parent shows his or her
child that of setting boundaries? Telling them right from wrong?
Restricting them? I'm sure you felt as a teenager that discipline
wasn't fun, but now as an adult and as a parent you realize it was an
expression of love and caring.

Walsch's *God* doesn't care. Does he meet the standard of the
New Age as a God of love? No, he is a *God* of indifference:

> **God:** You are living your life the way you are living your
> life, and I have no preference in the matter. This is the
> grand illusion in which you have engaged: that God *cares*
> one way or the other what you do. I do not care what you
> do, and that is hard for you to hear.[20]

If there is one thing we want God to tell us, it is that we can do
anything we want when it comes to sex. Walsch's *God* delivers:

> **God**: Put away your pointless taboos and restrictions upon sexual energy—rather, help others to truly understand its wonder, and to channel it properly. [21]

> **God**: But ... may sex be used for purposes of simple personal gratification? The surprising answer is yes—because "personal gratification" is another word for Self Love. [22]

Does *God* mean that the sex as described above is to be contained within the confines of marriage? According to Walsch's latest book, apparently not:

> My most romantic moments, by the way, were moments when I chose not to withhold anything.... I recall meeting a woman years ago at a party and looked right at her and said, "I want to go to bed with you. Sorry I have put it that way, but I only have about 5 minutes here." And she said, 'I wouldn't mind doing that with you, either.' And that was the most exciting weekend either of us had ever had ... We asked ourselves at the end of that weekend: Why can't we just do this all the time? By the way, we have never seen each other again since and we knew that we probably wouldn't. [23]

I think these last two conversations between Neale Donald Walsch and *God* sum it all up:

> **Walsch:** I've searched the path to God all my life.
> **God**: I know you have.
> **Walsch:** [A]nd now I've found it, and I can't believe it. It feels like I'm sitting here, writing this to myself.
> **God**: You are. [24]
> **God**: Come to Me along the path of your heart, not through a journey of your mind. You will never find Me in your mind. *In order to truly know God, you have to be out of your mind.* [25]

So does the *God* of these modern day New Age gurus exist? Is it true that the Christ Consciousness is in every human being? Is it accurate to say we all have God within and that He is an impersonal force making us feel warm and fuzzy inside but certainly does not tell us what to do? If you believe the Bible is the inspired Word of God, you know the answer to these questions. However, you may be surprised to find out these concepts about God have crept into our society and in particular the church—and the majority of Christian believers do not even see it happening.

Ancient Practices Brought Back To Life

[I]n almost all forms of the new mysticism there is a growing acceptance of the ideas of pantheism [everything is God]. The West and the East are coming together, and these pantheistic concepts are one of the strongest elements in the semantic mysticism of which we are speaking.[1]—Francis Schaeffer

One day I received an e-mail from a West Coast publisher, asking if I would be willing to review a book. I accepted the offer and when the book arrived, I started reading *A Time of Departing* by Ray Yungen.

The book described a style of praying I had never heard of before called *contemplative prayer.* As I continued to read I was struck by the similarities between an Eastern style of meditation like Transcendental Meditation and this contemplative prayer. The author wrote the book because he believed this style of prayer was infiltrating the church. I initially found that hard to believe and figured it must be a West Coast problem and certainly not a nationwide practice with which to be concerned. Although the author was right to warn the Christian community about this obvious Hindu prayer practice, certainly no pastor with any knowledge of Scripture would allow this in his church. I regarded it as a small problem—that is until I discovered it had already infiltrated local churches in my hometown, Minneapolis.

What a shock it was to learn how this style of prayer had become a standard practice in many churches across the nation. But it was even more disturbing that the pastoral leadership was welcoming it.

Many were actually defending it! I soon began to realize that many pastors had little knowledge of Eastern thought or its practices. What is contemplative prayer? When I first heard the term, I thought it sounded like a deep enriching practice of studying God's Word. The term seems to suggest taking a paragraph or phrase from the Bible and spending time thinking about it and contemplating its meaning. The dictionary describes the word contemplative as *calm and thoughtful, or inclined to be this way.* In this description, there is nothing wrong with contemplating God's Word.

However, the meaning described by Thomas Merton, Richard Foster, Brennan Manning and others who have actively promoted the *contemplative prayer movement* is a far cry from the dictionary meaning. New Age therapist Jacquelyn Small describes this type of prayer as Christian meditation. She states:

> Its practitioners are trained to focus on an inner symbol that quiets the mind.... When practitioners become skilled at this method of meditation, they undergo a deep trance state similar to auto-hypnosis.[2]

Jan Johnson, a spiritual director and retreat leader says this of the prayer style:

> *Contemplative prayer,* in its simplest form, is prayer in which you still your thoughts.... This puts you in a better state to be aware of God's presence, and it makes you better able to hear God's voice correcting, guiding, and directing you.[3]

Lectio Divina

The modern day contemplative prayer movement stems from the monastic period of Christianity (early middle ages), which was a time of experimentation and mystical practices. One of the practices, *lectio divina,* meaning *sacred reading,* involved taking a page of Scripture and reading it over and over again for the purpose of memorization. Some would describe this process as reading Scripture and then pondering it in solitude or silence, perhaps to read and then *chew on it* for a while.

However, Friar Luke Dysinger, a present-day monk at Saint Andrews Abbey, describes lectio divina in a different way:

> Choose a text of the Scriptures... Place yourself in a comfortable position and allow yourself to become silent. Some Christians focus for a few moments on their breathing; others have a beloved "prayer word" or "prayer phrase" they gently recite in order to become interiorly silent. For some the practice known as "centering prayer" makes a good, brief introduction to *lectio divina*....
>
> Then turn to the text and read it slowly, gently. Savor each portion of the reading, constantly listening for the "still, small voice" of a word or phrase that somehow says, "I am for you today...."
>
> Next take the word or phrase into yourself. Memorize it and slowly repeat it to yourself, allowing it to interact with your inner world of concerns, memories and ideas....
>
> Learn to use words when words are helpful, and to let go of words when they no longer are necessary. Rejoice in the knowledge that God is with you in both words and silence, in spiritual activity and inner receptivity.[4]

This practice has become extremely popular in today's Christian youth organizations and programs. Youth Specialties, a world renowned Christian organization, instructs young people and youth workers to incorporate lectio divina into their prayer lives. In their magazine, *Youth Worker Journal*, they describe lectio divina this way:

> This is a fancy Latin term for "sacred reading" and has also been called "meditation on the Word." Sacred reading is the practice of reading scripture slowly in a spirit of contemplation. The goal isn't exegesis or

analysis, but allowing God to speak to us through the word. Christians often refer to the Bible as God's love letter to mankind, and when we take the time to read it as such, we are practicing sacred reading[5]

The article then exhorts readers to:

Take a short passage and repeat it over and over again aloud. With each repetition, remove extraneous words until you've broken the passage down to one thought. An obvious example is John 14:27, which could easily be broken down to the word "peace."[6]

The concept of allowing God to speak through His Word is perfectly legitimate. I experience that when I read or meditate on the Bible. However, in the context of this article the purpose is not to contemplate the meaning of a Bible verse by thinking about it but is rather meant to gain an experience from it.

There is a difference between reading the Word and understanding its meaning versus a method of focusing on a single word to gain a mystical experience. Through Youth Specialties and many other youth-oriented organizations, our youth are being taught to treat the Bible as a meditative vehicle rather than a source of knowledge to further our understanding of God.

Youth Ministry & Spirituality Project (created by San Francisco Theological Seminary, in partnership with Youth Specialties and Sleepy Hollow Presbyterian Church[7]) embraces the contemplative life and teaches children and teens the basics of lectio divina. Please note that the steps below, while giving no direct instruction to repeat a mantra in order to enter the *silence*, closely parallel those of contemplative meditators. Youth Ministry & Spirituality Project presents a softened and subtle description, which will make the unfamiliar reader unaware of what is really being introduced. In short, the young participant is being groomed so as to make future instruction on mystical meditation more palatable. Read these steps and see how frightfully clever they really are:

Reading (lectio) - Slowly begin reading a biblical passage as if it were a long awaited love letter addressed to you. Approach it reverentially and expectantly, in a way that savors each word and phrase. Read the passage until you hear a word or phrase that touches you, resonates, attracts or even disturbs you.

Reflecting (meditatio) - Ponder this word or phrase for a few minutes. Let it sink in slowly and deeply until you are resting in it. Listen for what the word or phrase is saying to you at this moment in your life, what it may be offering to you, what it may be demanding of you.

Expressing (oratio) - When you feel ready, openly and honestly express to God the prayers that arise spontaneously within you from your experience of this word or phrase. These may be prayers of thanksgiving, petition, intercession, lament, or praise.

Resting (contemplatio) - Allow yourself to simply rest silently with God for a time in the stillness of your heart remaining open to the quiet fullness of God's love and peace. This is like the silence of communion between the mother holding her sleeping infant child or between lovers whose communication with each other passes beyond words.[8]

Why is it necessary to do this at all? For two thousand years, since Christ's ascension, His followers have been able to gain assurance of God's presence in their lives through the knowledge that He has risen and now dwells in their hearts. For the early church, there was no written word in wide circulation to "resonate," "attract" or "disturb" them. Throughout the centuries, faithful believers focused on the Word [who] became flesh and dwelt among us (John 1:14) rather than trying to find assurance through a single written word circulating through their minds.

By taking passages of Scripture, which have an intended meaning, and breaking them down into smaller, separate segments, often for the purpose of chanting over and over, the true meaning of the passages are lost. Rather a form of occult mysticism is practiced—with the hope and intention of gaining a mystical experience that God never intended when He gave the inspired words to His servants.

Hermits and Monastics

The practice of contemplative prayer came from the Desert Fathers of the monastic period. It is unknown whether the practice of lectio divina was distorted from an original practice of thoughtful reflection into a seeking to silence one's thoughts. Lectio divina may have started as a method of memorization and truly contemplating the meaning of the scriptures but then somehow turned into an Eastern style of repetitive meditation similar to Transcendental Meditation. Daniel Goldman, author of *Meditative Mind*, explains:

> The meditation practices and rules for living of these earliest Christian monks bear strong similarity to those of their Hindu and Buddhist renunciate brethren several kingdoms to the east. While Jesus and his teachings were their inspiration, the meditative techniques they adopted for finding their God suggest either a borrowing from the East or a spontaneous rediscovery. The ways of the Desert Fathers influence Christian monasticism to this day.[9]

Perhaps the Desert Fathers either came into contact with someone from the East who shared these practices with them, or maybe they stumbled across it themselves. Whatever its origin, this heretical practice has entered our churches virtually unopposed.

The first form of monasticism was practiced by the *hermit*. (In Greek the word means *desert*.)[10] The first hermit was St. Anthony, a revered Egyptian monk who moved away from society and into the desert around 270 A.D. Many followed St. Anthony's lifestyle and also became hermits. Nearly eighty years later the first monastery was built.[11] This brought the hermits together under one roof rather than each of them living alone in the desert.

As the centuries passed, Benedict brought order and discipline to the monastic life, laying the foundations for the most famous monastery in Europe, the motherhouse of the Benedictine Order. Benedict felt that each monastery should be self-contained and also self-supporting. Thus the monks wove their own cloth, made their own wine, and did their own carpentry and masonry. Benedictine monasteries swept throughout Western Europe and filled the European countryside.[12]

However, in the sixteenth century Martin Luther (once a monk himself) and other Reformers came against monasticism, saying that it "encourages the idea of two roads to God, a higher and a lower. But the gospel knows only one way to salvation. It is by faith alone in the Lord Jesus Christ."[13]

It was during the centuries of seeking solitude that Christian mysticism grew, but after monasticism faded so did Christian mysticism. The practices of lectio divina and contemplative prayer were, for the time being, forgotten. It would not be until the Council of Vatican II that the practice would be reintroduced to the world. The person most responsible for resurrecting contemplative prayer is none other than Thomas Merton.

Thomas Merton

Thomas Merton, a world-renowned Trappist monk and author, lived at the Abbey of Gethsemani near Bardstown, Kentucky from 1941 until his death in 1968. Merton was rooted in Catholicism, yet it is no secret that he sought the wisdom of other religions:

> Only three months before [his accidental death], he had begun his historic and long-hoped-for journey to the Far East, to give speeches, to meet with the Dalai Lama and to immerse himself in Buddhism and its keen insights into meditation.[14]

Fascinated with Eastern religions, he said:

> I believe that by openness to Buddhism, to Hinduism, and to these great Asian [mystical] traditions, we stand a wonderful chance of learning more about the potentiality of our own Christian traditions.[15]

What a strange thing for a *dedicated* Christian to say. Clearly, he did not realize Hinduism and Christianity stand on opposite poles. Merton's lack of understanding in his own religion, as well as others, is pronounced when he said:

> I see no contradiction between Buddhism and Christianity.... I intend to become as good a Buddhist as I can.[16]

Did Merton not see the difference? Apparently not!

Buddhism—Merton's Doorway to Mysticism

The opening to Eastern thought was made possible by the change in Vatican II. A decree named *Nostra Aetate* called upon the church to open a dialogue with people of different faiths:

> The Church therefore has this exhortation for her sons: prudently and lovingly, through dialogue and collaboration with the followers of other religions, and in witness of Christian faith and life, acknowledge, preserve, and promote the spiritual and moral goods found among these men, as well as the values in their society and culture.[17]

Wayne Teasdale, Ph.D. in Theology, a member of the North American Board for East-West Dialogue and a supporter of contemplative prayer, states:

> Buddhism, insofar as intermonastic exchange is concerned, had little contact with Christianity before the Council.... After the promulgation of *Nostra Aetate* contacts have become steadily more common. Prior to

the Council, Thomas Merton began his careful study of Taoism and Buddhism, particularly the Zen school. He spent ten years studying these traditions in depth and carrying on a long dialogue with D.T. Suzuki and other Buddhist masters. He was certainly ahead of his time in his own pilgrimage to the East. His encounter with the Dalai Lama after the Council in November 1968 has proven to be prophetic both for the church and monasticism, for it pointed the way to an important partner in dialogue, a dialogue which is now bearing fruit for both faiths and for all of humanity.[18]

Through his conversation with Eastern mystics, including the Dalai Lama, Thomas Merton began to see the similarities between Eastern meditation and contemplative prayer. However, instead of realizing that contemplative prayer had its roots in Eastern meditation and should therefore be avoided, he believed they were linked—a conviction that led him on the path to religious syncretism. Like many in the New Age who try to find ways to bring all religions together and to eschew the notion that only one ultimate truth about God exists, Merton embraced the same idea. By discovering that the same practice was being used in the East, it provided him the *proof* he so wanted that Christianity and Eastern thought were linked and perhaps had a similar origin.

However, the turning point in Merton's life came when he visited Sri Lanka:

Along with another priest, he visited the Buddhist shrine at Polonnaruwa but unlike the other priest who did not enter the actual shrine complex because of its "paganism," Merton took off his shoes and walked barefoot towards the enormous statues of the Buddha. What was about to happen to Merton was a pivotal, dramatic turning point of his life, a mystical moment for a Christian at a Buddhist shrine.

In Merton's own words, he describes the experience:

"Looking at these figures I was suddenly, almost forcibly, jerked clean out of the habitual, half-tied vision of things, and an inner clearness, clarity, as if exploding from the rocks themselves, became evident and obvious.

All problems are resolved and everything is clear. The rock, all matter, all life, is charged with dharmakaya... everything is emptiness and everything is compassion. I don't know when in my life I have ever had such a sense of beauty and spiritual validity running together in one aesthetic illumination."[19]

He had a supernatural spiritual experience. Through the constant practice of contemplative prayer it had opened his mind to Eastern thought. The conversion was complete.

The great irony of all this is that countless Asians of Buddhist and Hindu traditions have converted to Christianity over the years at great risk to their very lives. They abandoned their old ways because they saw irreconcilable differences with the Christian faith. Many were martyred for their new-found faith, and yet, Merton's life testifies how these new believers were unenlightened and their deaths unnecessary. If Merton is right, what must Jesus tell these martyrs when they meet Him in Heaven? If Merton is right, perhaps Jesus must apologize to them and say, "Sorry, but it was just a big joke. I wasn't really the only way to God."

What would be Merton's fruits after his *experience*? Would he try to convert Buddhists to Christianity? Would he try to convince them of the salvation promised only through Christ Jesus? What is absent from his biographies is the number of instances where he brought anyone to faith in Christ. Once Thomas Merton switched to religious syncretism his goal became *respecting* other beliefs in order to avoid any conflict. Did Merton spend the rest of his life trying to convince Buddhists and Hindus of their need for Jesus Christ? No, he did not. Rather, he chose to accommodate their beliefs, and by the end of his life, it was he who was converted to their way of thinking.

A Trojan Horse in the Church

Isn't it a pity that people are going into LSD to have spiritual experiences, when we have a tradition in the Church [contemplative prayer] which no one knows anything about?[1]—Thomas Merton

A Disciple of Thomas Merton

Richard Foster, presently the most influential and well-known of the *evangelical* contemplatives, considers Thomas Merton his mentor. Numerous times throughout his writings, Foster refers to his adoration and endorsement for Merton. In one book, he said Merton was the most influential spiritual director of the century.

Why would a Christian, after reading the works of Merton, ever want to endorse him and call him an influential spiritual director? Why would a Christian, after realizing Merton's allegiance to uniting Christianity with Buddhism, tell others to follow this man? While it is crystal clear that Merton's form of prayer and meditation was a compromising union of two utterly opposing beliefs, Richard Foster quotes him extensively and uses him as a guide to teach his readers on how to meditate.

In his book, *Spiritual Classics*, a compilation of what the book describes as the "Brightest lights of the Christian tradition," Foster speaks fondly of Merton and his beliefs:

> Thomas Merton has perhaps done more than any other twentieth-century figure to make the life of prayer widely known and understood.... His interest in contemplation led him to investigate prayer forms

in Eastern religion. Zen masters from Asia regarded him as the preeminent authority *on their kind* of prayer in the United States. (emphasis mine)[2]

Did Thomas Merton adhere to Buddhist and Hindu beliefs? Did he believe, as do Eastern religions and New Age proponents, that God is in everyone and everything ? Listen to his own words:

> It is a glorious destiny to be a member of the human race, … now I realize what we all are.… If only they [people] could all see themselves as they really are … I suppose the big problem would be that we would fall down and worship each other … At the center of our being is a point of nothingness which is untouched by sin and by illusions, a point of pure truth.… This little point … is the pure glory of God in us. It is in everybody.[3]

Wouldn't it have been a wonderful thing if Foster had written:

> Zen masters from Asia regarded Thomas Merton as the preeminent authority in their kind of prayer in the United States. It is unfortunate Merton was unable to recognize that because Eastern meditation and contemplative prayer are one and the same, therefore, both should be avoided. We should learn from Merton's mistakes and not engage in contemplative prayer.

But Foster doesn't say that. Instead, he encourages the body of Christ to cling to the teachings and practices of this man.

In the Thomas Merton chapter of *Spiritual Classics*, Richard Foster suggests the following exercise:

> 1. Choose a biblical text with rich content for contemplation.… Read it over peacefully and reflectively until a short phrase invites you deeper into prayer. Once you have "passed in" or "passed over"

through the text, relinquish the words and enter into wordless (or nearly wordless) prayer....

2. Consider using a visual focal point for contemplative prayer. A painting of the face of Jesus may serve in this way... An exquisite object, such as a rosebud (being a sign also of God's grandeur) may also serve as an entry point to contemplation.[4]

As I read the descriptions of how to engage in contemplative prayer they fall into three categories of methodology:

- Silence the mind by focusing on the breath.
- Silence the mind by the repetition of a word or phrase.
- Silence the mind by focusing on an object.

A Prayer That Requires Protection

What's the purpose of this type of prayer? Merton and Foster say it is to talk to God, to get closer to God or achieve union with God. And yet, because this method is not described or supported in Scripture (in fact, according to Matthew 6:7, vain repetitions are condemned), this is not really talking to God. It is a *subjective* experience and cannot be trusted. And if it isn't conversation with God, then with whom is it? I would propose that these *talks* with God are actually talks with demons. Curiously enough, Foster agrees.

In his book, *Prayer: Finding the Heart's True Home* Foster states:

> I also want to give a word of precaution. In the silent contemplation of God we are entering deeply into the spiritual realm, and there is such a thing as a supernatural guidance that is not divine guidance. While the Bible does not give us a lot of information on the nature of the spiritual world, we do know ... there are various orders of spiritual beings, and some of them are definitely not in cooperation with God and his way! ... But for now I want to encourage you to learn and practice prayers of protection.... "All dark and evil spirits must now leave."[5]

In this same book Richard Foster tells his readers:

> At the outset I need to give a word of warning, a little like the warning labels on medicine bottles. Contemplative prayer is not for the novice. I do not say this about any other form of prayer. All are welcome, regardless of proficiency or expertise, to enter freely into adoration and meditation and intercession and a host of other approaches to prayer. But contemplation is different. While we are all equally precious in the eyes of God, we are not all equally ready to listen to "God's speech in his wondrous, terrible, gentle, loving, all embracing silence."[6]

Really? Why would God ask us to become involved in a type of prayer that could bring exposure and harm from demonic influences? Foster warns that a novice Christian should not engage in it. But where in Scripture is such a notion supported? Is there such a hierarchy in Christianity?

While it is certainly true that it takes time to truly understand God's Word and apply it to all areas of our life (a process that can span a lifetime), the method to maturity is studying and understanding God's Word while learning to follow and obey His commandments—not practicing mind-blanking exercises and prayers that, in order to even pray them, need special protection from demons.

Why would Foster or any believer want to practice such a form of prayer? Could it be they are infatuated with the seductive feeling that accompanies it—and like other contemplatives, feel the need to get closer to God? But this presents a dilemma, for it is the finished work of Christ on the Cross that allows us access to the throne of God, and that access is immediately available to us the moment we are born-again. It is not just for an elite group of people who are "mature" enough to handle it; no, it is for all who have been born of the Spirit and justified by faith.

> But Christ came as High Priest of the good things to come, with the greater and more perfect tabernacle

not made with hands, that is, not of this creation. Not with the blood of goats and calves, but with His own blood He entered the Most Holy Place once for all, having obtained eternal redemption. (Hebrews 9: 11, 12)

Jesus our High Priest has brought us as close to God as we can get until He returns. We draw near to God only by faith and through the finished work of Christ. For those who have never been born-again, I can understand their desperation for the *feeling* of being close to God. Those who are born-again do not need that for the Spirit within them calls out Abba Father—they are sheep and they know the voice of the Shepherd: "My sheep hear My voice, and I know them, and they follow Me" (John 10:27).

Mind-altering mysticism cannot bring us closer to God.[7] Perhaps those who feel the need for contemplative prayer, as taught by Richard Foster, Thomas Merton and other contemplatives, feel an emptiness in their walk with the Lord because they do not understand Scripture and the great power that lies within its truth.

In reality, contemplative spirituality is a works-based, religious philosophy. *We* have to be the initiate. *We* have to do something to get God's attention. And yet Scripture is clear—it is by grace we are saved, not by works. And using mystical methods to get His attention is heresy and an utter insult to Christ's finished work on the Cross.

Which Jesus Are You Talking To?

Contemplative prayer is not the only type of meditation Foster endorses. Listen to portions of this exercise that he tells his readers to engage in:

In *your imagination*, picture yourself walking along a lovely forest path. Take your time … After observing yourself for a bit, take the perspective of the one walking, rather than the one observed. Try to feel the breeze upon your face … ponder the beauty of flowers and birds. When you are able to experience the scene with all your senses, the path breaks out onto a lovely grassy knoll.... After exploring the meadow for a time, lie down on your back looking up at blue sky and white clouds.... Thank the Lord for the beauty.

After awhile there is a deep yearning within to go into the *upper regions* beyond the clouds. In your *imagination* allow your spiritual body, shining with light, to *rise out of your physical body*.... [S]ee yourself lying in the grass and reassure your body that *you will return* momentarily. Imagine your spiritual self, alive and vibrant, rising up through the clouds and into the stratosphere. Observe your physical body, the knoll, and the forest shrink as you leave the earth. *Go deeper and deeper* into outer space until there is nothing except the warm presence of the eternal Creator. Rest in His presence. Listen quietly.... Note carefully any instruction given. With time and experience you will be able to distinguish readily between mere human thought that may bubble up to the conscious mind and the True Spirit which inwardly moves upon the heart.... When it is time for you to leave, audibly thank the Lord for His goodness and return to the meadow. Walk joyfully back along the path until you return home full of new life and energy. (emphasis mine)[8]

When I was introduced to astral projection or out of body meditations during my New Age years, there was a plethora of books or guided-imagery tapes to choose from. These guided-imagery meditations were advertised to reduce stress. However, the majority of them were used to assist the soul in reaching out into the heavens to feel the love of the Universe that ties all things together. Ahhhh.

As I read this meditation by Richard Foster, I was dismayed at the striking similarities between it and the many in which I had engaged in during the past. Foster attempts to cover himself from criticism by writing in the footnotes:

Over the years since the publication of *Celebration of Discipline* some have asked if I am endorsing astro-travel or astral projection in this meditation exercise.

My answer is, "No, decidedly not!" This meditation is only an aid for our centering down [contemplative prayer], nothing more.[9]

Foster states that he is not endorsing astral projection, but how is one able to discern between the *real* astral projection and the one he describes? I can't tell the difference and I used to do it. How could one know that the God met in the stratosphere is the God of the Bible? Contemplatives have an answer for that—*Intent!* As long as the intent of the heart is to find Jesus through this meditation technique or contemplative prayer, then that is what will be found. No questions asked! However, what if the intent is to find Buddha, will this method work or is it only reserved for Christians?

Tilden Edwards, another contemplative and the founder of the pantheistic Shalem Institute for Spiritual Formation in Washington, DC, states, "What makes a particular practice Christian is not its source, but its *intent.*"[10] By this standard, I could use a Ouija board to communicate with Jesus. How would I know that the Jesus I am speaking to is the real Jesus? I don't. The experience is subjective. I had an experience. It was real. It was good. Therefore, it must be God. That was the same reasoning I developed when I performed psychic readings.

Foster describes the first steps of meditation. "The inner world of meditation is most easily entered through the door of the imagination. We fail today to appreciate its tremendous power."[11] How does he know that the God in his imagination he is speaking to is the real God? He doesn't!

In II Corinthians 11: 3, 4 the apostle Paul is worried about Christians being led astray by false prophets and Satan himself. He states:

> But I fear, lest somehow, as the serpent deceived Eve by his craftiness, so your minds may be corrupted from the simplicity that is in Christ. For if he who comes preaches another Jesus whom we have not preached, or if you receive a different spirit which you have not

received, or a different gospel which you have not
accepted—you may well put up with it!

In other words you might just accept the words of Foster because many pastors also do so. The demons of the spirit world have
been practicing deception for centuries, and they know how to disguise themselves as angels, God, Jesus or the Holy Spirit. And according to I Corinthians 11:15, they come as ministers of righteousness:

> Now the Spirit expressly says that in latter times some
> will depart from the faith, giving heed to deceiving
> spirits and doctrines of demons. (I Timothy 4:1)

How sadly prophetic this Bible verse is.

Spiritual Directors

According to Spiritual Directors International, spiritual
direction is:

> ...the art of Christian listening carried out in the context of a
> one-to-one trusting relationship. It is when one Christian is
> trained to be a competent guide who then
> "companions" another person, listening to that
> person's life story with an ear for the movement of
> the Holy, of the Divine.[12]

Across the globe, *spiritual directors*[13] *are* multiplying at an incredible rate. If indeed these directors are hearing from the one true
God, then we can assume that the thousands, if not millions, of
people being directed are receiving godly wisdom. However, if the
majority of spiritual directors are not hearing from God but rather
from demonic influences, then what type of wisdom are they im-
parting to these multitudes of people?

As a New Ager, I would listen to the voices of my spirit guides
during my daily meditations, then frequently seek out guidance and
understanding from my teacher. Her objective was to help me divine (from divination) God's will. While cautious not to inject her

own feelings or interpretations and not wanting to interfere with the information from my spirit guides, through her questioning she helped me to discern the message.

When I first heard the term spiritual director as a Christian, I saw how these Christian directors had the same purpose as my former directors. When a Christian practices contemplative prayer, he seeks out a spiritual director in order to interpret the message he receives during his time in the silence.

Listen to this *description from a woman who has hired a spiritual director to help her through her contemplative prayer session:

> Her palms open heavenward, Helene sets them on the couch by her thighs and then starts with a prayer. On occasion, she rings a brass bell to separate the clamor from the quiet. Sometimes she lights a candle, as if to remind us that the Holy Spirit is with us, interceding on our behalf with words we don't even know how to find.
>
> For the next two or three hours, Helene listens intently with me for God's voice. I pay her $30 for this priceless gift. We sit in her sunroom, chatting about my everydayness: the job, the migraines, the mother, the husband, the sex, the prayer life, the joys, the mistakes. Sometimes we read Scripture; in it we find people with the same concerns as mine. In it all, I slowly notice God beckoning.
>
> Helene isn't a mystic or a saint. The title I use for her— spiritual director—isn't helpful, either. As any decent spiritual director is quick to say, the term's a misnomer. Helene doesn't tell me what to do or try to answer questions only God can answer. In her sunroom, we listen for—and sometimes hear—the Holy Ghost.
>
> Once, as I and my biological clock neared 28, I came to her distraught over my feelings of inadequacy as mother

---

*Reprinted by permission from *Today's Christian Woman* magazine (September/ October 2004), published by *Christianity Today International* Carol Stream, Illinois.

material. "Have you talked to God about it?" Helene asked. "Not yet," I replied. "Why don't we ask him now what he thinks," she proposed. She prayed for guidance, and we sat in silence for about five minutes.

There was nothing I wanted more than to hear God's words of comfort. But as the minutes flew by, I felt—pardon the expression—spiritually constipated, unable to discern God's voice. I finally gave up trying. As soon as I did, a thought popped into my head: *You can't make this happen!* I suddenly realized that just as I couldn't make God answer my questions immediately, I couldn't resolve my feelings toward motherhood when I wanted to. Both require waiting—but would be resolved in time. When I conveyed this to Helene, she said, "See, there's your answer."[14]

The spiritual director's reply to this woman reminds me of when I used to think I could read people's auras, when in reality I was just observing what was already there. While I certainly understand this woman's frustration in wanting to receive guidance and wisdom from God with the help of a spiritual director, hasn't that been the plight of man since Adam and Eve were cast out of the garden? No one has the corner on hearing God's voice, and that's why God gave us His written Word through the Apostles and Prophets to help us discern His will, with the Holy Spirit quickening to us the truth of His Word.

With regard to spiritual directors, a few questions must be answered. First of all, why does the contemplative Christian need one? According to an article in *Christianity Today*, spiritual direction is defined as:

> ...a voluntary relationship between a person who seeks to grow in the Christian life and a director. The latter is not, notice, a counselor or therapist. Rather, he or she is a mature Christian who helps the directee both to discern what the Holy Spirit is doing and saying and to act ι that discernment, drawing nearer to God in Christ.[15]

Apparently there is a need for guidance for the contemplative when venturing into this spiritual realm. Richard Foster warns:

> So that we may not be led astray, however, we must understand that we are not engaging in some flippant work. We are not calling on some cosmic bellhop. It is serious and even dangerous business.[16]

So if we are going to practice entering the silence, we need spiritual directors to protect us.

But this leads us to another question: Would God put us into a position of wading through the darkness of a spiritual realm where spiritual beings are not in cooperation with God? Contemplatives, such as Richard Foster, admit that contemplative prayer is dangerous because it opens one up to demonic entities. In order to engage in this practice, you must be a mature Christian as to not be misled by the voices conjured up during this practice. This is where the need for spiritual directors arises. However, is there any place in Scripture that sanctions our navigating through the dark spiritual world then seeking out a spiritual director or medium for guidance and understanding? I think not.

Finally, we must ask ourselves the most important question of all: Are these Christian spiritual directors truly hearing from God? In order to effectively answer that question let's take a look at a few of these spiritual directors.

Ruth Haley Barton

Ruth Haley Barton, a former staff member of Willow Creek Community Church and trained at the Shalem Institute for Spiritual Formation, promotes contemplative prayer to such an extent that she left Willow Creek to form her own organization, The Transforming Center. Her goal is to teach as many people as possible the practice of contemplative prayer. Needless to say, she is a devotee of Richard Foster and Thomas Merton. While on staff as a spiritual director at Willow Creek, Ms. Barton co-authored a spiritual-formation curriculum.

She states in this curriculum:

> A few years ago, I began to recognize an inner chaos
> in my soul.... I sought out a spiritual director, someone
> well versed in the ways of the soul.... [The spiritual
> director] said to me, ... "What you need is stillness
> and silence."[17]

She describes the process of contemplative prayer in this way:

> Ask for a simple prayer to express your willingness to
> meet God in *the silence*.... a simple statement ... such as
> "Here I am...." Help yourself return to your original
> intent by repeating the prayer that you have chosen.[18]

Ms. Barton shares her technique of contemplative prayer to
aid in finding the silence:

> Identify your sacred space and time. Explore all
> the possibilities for a time and physical space in which
> you can be alone on a regular basis.

> Begin with a modest goal ... Ten, fifteen or twenty
> minutes of time spent in actual silence ...

> Choose a prayer phrase that expresses your desire or need
> for God ... It is best if the prayer is not more than six or
> eight syllables so that it can be prayed very naturally in
> the rhythm of your breathing. Pray this prayer several
> times as an entry into silence and also as a way of dealing
> with distractions.

> [S]imply let them [distractions] go ... repeating the
> prayer you have chosen. Use your prayer phrase for as
> long as it captures what is most true about your hearts
> desire for God, and link it with a body posture that also
> helps you express your spiritual desire.[19]

Ms. Barton was trained at the Shalem Institute for Spiritual Formation under Tilden Edwards. In her book, *Invitation to Solitude and Silence, Experiencing God's Transforming Presence*, she makes a biblical error immediately. She introduces the reader to her underlying theme, which is the story of Elijah's flight from Jezebel where he meets the Lord at Mount Sinai.

She references the *New Revised Standard Version* of the Bible:

> At that place he came to a cave, and spent the night there. Then the Word of the LORD came to him, saying, "What are you doing here, Elijah?"

> He answered, "I have been very zealous for the LORD, the God of hosts; for the Israelites have forsaken your covenant, thrown down your altars, and killed your prophets with the sword. I alone am left, and they are seeking my life, to take it away." He said, "Go out and stand on the mountain before the LORD, for the LORD is about to pass by." Now there was a great wind, so strong that it was splitting mountains and breaking rocks in pieces before the LORD, but the LORD was not in the wind; and after the wind an earthquake, but the LORD was not in the earthquake; and after the earthquake a fire, but the LORD was not in the fire; and after the fire a sound of sheer silence.

> When Elijah heard it, he wrapped his face in his mantle and went out and stood at the entrance of the cave. Then there came a voice to him that said, "What are you doing here, Elijah?" (1 Kings 19: 9-13)

Ruth Haley Barton uses this translation to prove that contemplative prayer is referred to in Scripture. She uses this line to prove it: "and after the fire *a sound of sheer silence.*" However, this translation does not describe silencing the mind in any way.

When Elijah heard what? A sound of sheer silence? That got him out to the entrance of the cave? No other translation uses that phrase in that way.

In the *New American Standard Bible* it states, "...and after the fire *a sound of a gentle blowing.* In the *New King James Version*, it states, "And after the fire came a gentle whisper." In Hebrew the term says, "*The tone of a gentle blowing.*" That is what Elijah heard. Ms. Barton uses this story to share with her readers that Elijah went to the mountains to seek silence and solitude and to talk to God. However, her misuse of Scripture would suggest either her ignorance or her desperation to prove that the Bible references contemplative prayer, when in fact, it does not.

How could one derive from this story any reference to silencing the mind in order to hear God speak? Who initiated the conversation with Elijah? It was the Lord. The Bible never describes Elijah performing a ritual to get God to speak to him. Rather it was the priests of Baal opposing Elijah who used a ritual of repetition (I Kings 18:26).

What is the purpose for this silence that Merton, Foster and Barton so desperately seek? Last year, I was invited to a conference at a beautiful retreat center tucked away in the Appalachian Mountains. I was struck by the beauty and the quietness of the location. In the evening after the conference was over, I adjourned to my room. The hotel room was unique in that it had no television and no radio. The purpose was clear—to allow guests time in solitude and in prayer and to leave the distractions of the world behind. I spent many hours reading Scripture and pondering its meaning for me.

Throughout the evening I paced the room, asking God for His continued guidance and thinking out loud how God was directing my path. I read aloud Scripture to reinforce its meaning. I was, in a sense, preaching the Word to myself.

Afterwards I felt confident God was present in my life. I was moved by the thought of His sacrifice on the Cross for me. His words, which are communicated throughout the Bible, gave me comfort and peace.

Never during this time did I silence my thoughts. His written Word cried out to me. The verses of the Bible rumbled like thunder in my heart. His Word called to me loudly and clearly. They set me on the path of His will for me, not my own. All this was accomplished without seeking the silence, without centering down, without breath prayer, and without contemplative prayer.

Ms. Barton ends her book, *Invitation to Solitude and Silence* in this way:

> After Elijah had been in solitude for quite sometime, God asked him again, "What are you doing here, Elijah?"...
>
> Elijah was still in a state that clearly indicated that he needed to make some changes in his life. In response to Elijah's condition, God graciously responded with some very specific instructions.... This guidance seemed to come not so much because Elijah asked for guidance but rather as a natural result of the fact that he had gotten quiet enough to hear.[20]

The lesson? If you quiet your mind you will hear God talking to you also. You are going to receive instruction and guidance—all because you waited in your mind or silenced your mind so that God would speak. Is Ms. Barton able to discern God's voice from that of a demon's?

Ms. Barton totally misses the point of the story of Elijah. Elijah's accomplishment, after an overwhelming miracle through God, was the defeat of the prophets of Baal. He demonstrated to the pagan worshippers of Baal that it was the Lord God of Abraham who was the one true God. If Ms. Barton truly wanted to be more like Elijah, she would be demanding that the pagan practice of contemplative prayer be banished from the church.

Tilden Edwards

In the back of Richard Foster's book, *Celebration of Discipline*, there is a list of books which Foster calls, "excellent books on spirituality." Among those listed is a book titled *Spiritual Friend* by Tilden Edwards.[21] Foster says that *Spiritual Friend* helps clear away confusion. In this book, Edwards states that contemplative prayer is the bridge between Western Christianity and Eastern spirituality.[22] And on a website newsletter, *Jesus and Buddha: Good Friends,* Edwards describes the *similarities* he sees between Jesus and Buddha:

> For many years, I have kept in my office an ink drawing of two smiling figures with their arms around each other: Jesus Christ and Gautama Buddha, with the caption: "Jesus and Buddha must be very good friends." They are not the same, but they are friends, not enemies, and they are not indifferent to one another. From the very beginning of Shalem [Institute for Spiritual Formation], I have been moved to affirm that statement....
>
> In their *contemplative strands,* each tradition shares in its own way a basic stance of compassionate "presence to what is ... Particular Buddhist practices that I have experienced in the last 26 years have, with grace, shown me such an "inclusive" mind....
>
> [P]erhaps we should no longer speak of interfaith relations but of *intrafaith relations* as we come to realize that we share the *same mysterious divine ground* with different, evolving experiences of it. *Contemplative traditions* can be particularly helpful in showing us the *inclusive ground* that is deeper than words, structures and categories; a holy ground that is finally trust-worthy, liberating, and pervaded by a mysterious love ever drawing us. (emphasis mine)[23]

One of the disturbing similarities I find when reading any of the contemplatives' writings is the strange admiration for Eastern faiths. Although I understand how we as Christians should be mindful and polite to people of other faiths, it cannot be to the extent of an accommodation or an acceptance to their view of God, where the significance of the Cross is undermined as the only means of salvation through God's one and only Son.

Edwards makes this assertion:

> In the wider ecumenism of the Spirit being opened for
> us today, we need to humbly accept the learnings of
> particular Eastern religions.... What makes a particular
> practice Christian is not its source, but its intent ... this
> is important to remember in the face of those Christians
> who would try to impoverish our spiritual resources by
> too narrowly defining them. If we view the human
> family as one in God's spirit, then historical cross-
> fertilization is not surprising ... selective attention to
> Eastern practices can be of a great assistance to a fully
> embodied Christian life.[24]

We as Christians must humbly accept the "learnings" of Eastern religions? Why? What do they offer? Salvation? Truth? Forgiveness of sin? And yet, Edwards labels criticizers as those who wish
to impoverish spiritual resources by too narrowly defining them.

That would have to include Jesus also when He said, "Enter by
the narrow gate; for wide is the gate and broad is the way that leads
to destruction, and there are many who go in by it." (Matthew 7:13).

The results of the contemplatives constant search for similarities with the Eastern spirituality is not to bridge the gap so that we
may better communicate the truth of Christ, but rather to bring us
all together under one faith. Edwards enthusiastically embraces
the contemplative movement and how it has opened his mind to
Buddhism. Edwards seeks the wide gate, but alas this gate only
leads to destruction and unfortunately, he will take many with him.

Brennan Manning

Brennan Manning, popular author and lecturer, is one of the
more influential within the contemplative community and is
particularly admired by young people. He has written several
books—*Gentle Revolutionaries, The Ragamuffin Gospel, Signature of Jesus*
and *Abba's Child* just to name a few.

Among the themes within the New Age community is the one
stating that God and man are not separate—they are one. Here
Manning echoes this theme in *The Gentle Revolutionaries:*

A Trojan Horse in the Church 159

The Christian has broken through the illusion of duality and separation, and his Spirit-filled consciousness has created a world that is saturated with beauty, lucidity, vividness and intensity. The programmed addictions that dominated his attention and directed his concentration have disappeared into the nothingness of non-attention.

The dualistic split between consciousness and spirit is woven into a single tapestry, and he begins to perceive all people and all things in a unitive framework. Maloney writes, "Whatever the person is doing, opening or closing his eyes, he finds the Divine Presence everywhere in the unity of all things, and this forces the person out of himself in a spirit of worship and service.... It is an experience of God at the heart of the matter. He loves this being, this person, this tree, this stone and God at the same time. There is no moving from this to that, but in his vision he sees at one and the same time the created being and the infinite love of God who creates this being and gives him as a gift. He finds the gift and the Giver in the same look."[25]

He quotes George Maloney who lectures on prayer, Eastern Christian spirituality, modern psychology, and yoga and draws upon the writings of Eastern mystics. Manning has no difficulties with this person's background or his beliefs because they are essentially the same as his own.

Read any of the contemplatives; without a doubt, their writings are filled with mysticism—thus the term *Christian mysticism*. I find this term troubling. It reminds me of the oxymoron in George Carlin's joke *jumbo shrimp*. Mysticism is defined as, "An immediate knowledge of God attained in this present life through a personal religious experience."[26] We are again faced with a subjective experience that *we* initiate to gain an intimate knowledge of God.

Manning regards his experience in contemplative prayer as more relevant than anything found in Scripture:

> I am deeply distressed by what I only can call in our Christian culture the idolatry of the Scriptures. For many Christians, the Bible is not a pointer to God but God himself. In a word—bibliolatry. God cannot be confined within the covers of a leather-bound book. I develop a nasty rash around people who speak as if mere scrutiny of its [the Bible] pages will reveal precisely how God thinks and precisely what God wants.[27]

In one respect, I understand what Manning is saying in that a Christian could make a leather-bound Bible into an idol itself. But that is not why Christians hold the Bible in the highest regard—rather it is because God has written the words it contains. What other authority is there? God is not contained by a leather-bound book, but the knowledge He chooses to reveal to us is. The secrets or mysteries God withholds from us are what the contemplatives strive to know. They feel that by entering into this spiritual realm, or sacred space as many refer to it, God will reveal those mysteries to them.

Manning so believes in what he teaches that he thinks the only way to have an intimate knowledge of God is through contemplative/centering prayer. He states:

> The tragedy in the Church today is that we have confused beliefs and faith, doctrines and lived experience. Contemplative prayer bridges the gap between belief and experience because it is the bridge of faith. It teaches what theology alone could never convince us of—that God is love."[28]

The study of God through reading the Bible could never convince me that God is love? The story of His death on the Cross isn't proof enough? I understand that knowledge alone may not convince everyone, but isn't knowing that we have received the Holy Spirit because of God's promises enough? The knowledge that I am cleansed of my sins is enough for me to feel the warmth of God's love forever. Knowing that He came to die for me is my proof. I do not need contemplative prayer to bridge the gap.

Apparently this isn't enough for Manning. He states that we must grab hold of God. "'Grabbing aholt' of God is the goal of contemplative prayer."[29] I must grab God. I must demand His presence. God *must* be at *my* beck and call. I wasn't aware that God was so busy that I needed to grab Him to get His attention.

According to Brennan Manning, how do we get God's attention? Consider his words:

> [T]he first step in faith is to stop thinking about God at the time of prayer.[30]

> Choose a single, sacred word or phrase that captures something of the flavor of your intimate relationship with God. A word such as Jesus, Abba, Peace, God or a phrase such as "Abba, I belong to you."... Without moving your lips, repeat the sacred word inwardly, slowly, and often.[31]

> When distractions come, ... simply return to listening to your sacred word.... [G]ently return [your mind] to your sacred word.[32]

According to Manning and his contemplative colleagues, I'm doing things all wrong. First, I am ruining my prayer time by thinking about God. Second, I am not repeating God's name over and over again in my brain. Is it true that God cannot hear me unless I repeat His name fifty times? I would think after hearing His name repeated that many times, the first words I would hear from God might be "Enough already Brian! I may have been around before time, but I'm not deaf!" Incidentally, those same distractions that I experienced when I was practicing TM are eliminated by coincidentally the same practice: "Gently return your mind to your sacred word." How much time each day does Manning recommend we perform contemplative prayer? Two twenty-minute periods each day—coincidentally the same amount prescribed in TM.

Contemplative Prayer and TM—Too Much in Common

The similarities between TM and contemplative prayer are quite remarkable. In both disciplines the goal is to achieve silence or that sacred space. With TM the goal is to silence the thoughts so a oneness with the universe can be achieved. In other words, get closer to God or the universal energy that connects us all. The goal of contemplative prayer is also to get closer to *God*. Each uses a word, phrase or mantra to achieve the silence. Each uses a word, phrase or mantra as a means to push away any thoughts.

The only difference is the word chosen. But does that make any difference?

When I began TM, I was given a mantra (mantra in Sanskrit means *to be liberated from thought*). I was told that every person had his or her very own mantra. No one else in the world had the same word. However, years later I learned the truth—during court proceedings with a lawsuit brought against the Maharishi, they were required to reveal all the TM mantras. Instead of unique mantras made for each person, they admitted there were only sixteen mantras, all assigned based upon age.[33]

- eng   0-11 years old
- em   12-13
- enga   14-15
- ema   16-17
- ieng   18-19
- iem   20-21
- ienga   22-23
- iema   24-25
- shirim   26-29
- shiring 30-34
- kirim   35-39
- kiring   40-44
- hirim   45-49
- hiring   50-54
- sham   55-59
- shama   60 +

All that time, I thought my word was just mine. *Was* I ever fooled, in more ways than one! I thought the word had some sort of magical element to it. Studies conducted to prove whether TM actually achieved some of the claims it purported to address (i.e., lowering blood pressure, lowering of the heart rate, reducing stress), revealed something quite interesting:

> The most devastating evidence against the unique characteristic of TM mantras was presented by ... Herbert Benson, [M.D.].
>
> Benson's impressive historical analyses of mystical states demonstrated that verbal repetition was a key portion of the process.... instructing subjects to relax for a twenty-minute period and to repeat the number "one."... the physiological and psychological changes obtained were almost identical to the alleged effects of repeating the TM mantra.[34]

The conclusion? It didn't matter what the repeated word was! Whether a TM mantra was chanted or the word *one*, or even the word *Jesus*, the results were the same. Those results? An altered state of consciousness.

The Kundalini Effect

On a pro-contemplative spirituality web site, I came across the descriptions of those who had experienced the effect of contemplative prayer. Some of this is very disturbing and should be read with care:

> I have been practicing Centering Prayer for 2 ½ years.... I began experiencing Kundalini-like symptoms three months after beginning the practice. They were quite intense at first. They have continued in various forms since then. Lately, I only experience them at the very beginning of prayer. I am not aware of any other moral manifestations. Father Keating [see chapter 11] advised

me personally to ignore them if I could, and if they were too bothersome to "balance the energy" with physical exercise or a yoga practice.—**Gary**

I began to feel energy or electrical current rushes through my body, and some stomach muscle cramping. For the next few weeks, these sensations intensified, and bodily shaking/twitching began, lasting from several seconds to perhaps 5 or 10 minutes. A mild euphoria accompanied. I could willfully stop these sensations, but instead prayed fervently to Christ to help lead me away from them if they were not efficacious to his will.... After meditation, I am left with a tingly face and neck (sometimes arms) and a full or pressured feeling inside my crown. In recent weeks, I am getting more release as the energy eventually gently fizzes out of the top of my head.... Also, euphoric energy flows come [and go].—**Richard**

Other effects Richard described included:

- Body frequently vibrating.

- Energy from fingers or palms can be felt on face, arm or leg,—a buzzing cool/warm breeze.

- Energy ridges around the body.

- When people are close to me—even my back— as when shopping, I get a sense of a different energy field entering mine, and they all feel different.

- Bringing a palm within a foot from my heart chakra is like physically squeezing it, and can actually make me cry.[35]

What these two men were experiencing is called Kundalini meditation or the Kundalini effect. Symptoms can include headaches, nausea, tingling sensation, and uncontrollable twitching. The Sanskrit word *Kundalini* means the *curled one*, and is also called Kundalini awakening or the awakening of the serpent. Practitioners describe it as a curled channel in the tailbone area.[36] It can rise through the chakras (psychic centers situated along the spine from the tailbone to the top of the head), creating physical symptoms ranging from sensations of heat and tremors to involuntary laughing or crying, talking in tongues, nausea, diarrhea or constipation, rigidity or limpness, and animal-like movements and sounds.

A variety of spiritual practices can bring on the Kundalini effect as described here:

> A Kundalini release can be triggered by erroneous meditation, yoga, breathing exercises, reiki, qigong healing, tantra, transcendental meditation and other eastern or new age spiritual exercises. When the Kundalini energy is rising through the chakras, it can cause big problems for the bodily and mental health. We have got hundreds of e-mails from people around the world who have been damaged by these artificial spiritual exercises.[37]

Other Kundalini symptoms include:

- Burning hot or ice cold streams moving up the spine.
- Pains in varying locations throughout the body.
- Vibrations, unease, or cramps in legs and other parts of body.
- Fast pulse and increased metabolism.
- Disturbance in the breathing—and/or heart function.
- Sensitivity to sound, light, smell, and proximity of other people.
- Mystical/religious experiences.
- Parapsychological abilities.
- Persistent anxiety or anxiety attacks, confusion
- Insomnia, manic high spirits or deep depression. Energy loss.
- Impaired concentration and memory.
- Total isolation due to inability to communicate inner

experiences out.

- Experiences of possession and poltergeist phenomena.[38]

I mention these symptoms because they can happen in both Kundalini meditation and contemplative prayer meditation. Cassandrah Batya, who as a Christian, decided to practice contemplative meditation because she wanted to *feel* a closer relationship with God. However, the more she got into contemplative spirituality, the worse things got. Listen to excerpts of her candid and compelling testimony:

> My spiritual focus and prayer became less about Jesus, and more about mystical spiritual highs and insights. Contemplative spirituality became my drug.
>
> During prayer, a voice in the back of my head would tell me I was a witch.
>
> One night, my thumb/hand began to shake on its own during prayer.
>
> By nature, I am a kind and loving person and have been told such, but I started to have hateful and venomous mood swings and became at moments verbally abusive to my loved ones. I was surprised at my own behavior and language.[39]

Eventually she realized she had entered a dangerous demonic realm. After conducting her own research she discovered the symptoms she experienced were the same as the Kundalini effect. Immediately, she began praying for guidance:

> I repented and renounced all contemplative practices, inner/esoteric spirituality, and mysticism. Actually, I wept aloud, fell on my knees, and begged God's forgiveness. I threw out all books and music that dealt with mystics, mysticism, and esoteric/inner/

contemplative spirituality and anything else related to it. I immediately knew I had done the right thing. The atmosphere in my home changed, and for the first time in a long time, when I prayed to God I felt a peace and joy in my heart, and not great fear or terror.[40]

Does it not ever occur to proponents of contemplative prayer that there might be something wrong with this practice? Sadly, the answer is usually no.

Imagine a health food store that recommends arsenic as a healthy supplement and when they receive complaints from people describing stomach cramps, headaches and nausea they just tell their customers to ignore these things. Ridiculous you say? Right. But that is exactly what those experiencing the Kundalini effect are often told by their spiritual directors. And such advice is utterly beyond ridiculous.

Prayer or a Self-Induced Consciousness?

Matthew Fox, a self-described liberal theologian whose views are aligned closely with the New Age, states in an interview referring to the subject of contemplative prayer:

> I wrote to Thomas Merton about this in 1967 and he said, "Isn't it a pity that people are going into LSD to have spiritual experiences, when we have a tradition [contemplative prayer] in the Church which no one knows anything about?"[41]

Merton made that statement because he knew that LSD brings one into an altered state of consciousness. What an incredible admission! An LSD hallucinogenic trip or practicing contemplative prayer—both give the same effect—an altered state of consciousness. Why would any Christian who has a personal relationship with Jesus Christ need to go into an altered state of consciousness to speak with God? We do not, and to do so is perilous and may I suggest an insult to the Lord.

In Ray Yungen's book *A Time of Departing*, Yungen states:

> The premise here is that God can never be known in a conventional non-mystical way. Therefore, the mind has to be *shut down, turned off* so one can enter the cloud of unknowing where the presence of God awaits....
>
> Legitimate mysticism was always initiated *by* God to certain individuals for certain revelations and was never based on a method for the changing of consciousness. In Acts [11:5], Peter fell into a trance while in prayer. But it was God, not Peter, who initiated the trance and facilitated it.
>
> A mystic, on the other hand, is someone who uses rote methods in an attempt to meet God. Those who use this method put themselves in a trance without God's sanction. This approach is extremely dangerous.[42]

The Achille's heel of contemplative prayer is its lack of scriptural support. Throughout the last ten years I have spent countless hours reading New Age authors who use the Bible for their own means. They often quote from the Bible out of context because the actual meaning wouldn't serve their purposes.

In Anthony Robbins book *Awaken The Giant Within*, he quotes from the Gospel of John 1:1, "In the beginning was the word..." He then uses that phrase to make this point:

> It is important to realize that words shape our beliefs; they impact our actions. If we want to change our lives, ... we need to consciously select the words we're going to use.[43]

That is not what John meant. The Word was God, not an actual word.

Many of the contemplative authors take Scripture out of context. Robbins is not a professing Christian and therefore is somewhat excused. But those claiming to be Christians should know better.

Listen to how Richard Foster has taken the word silence and twisted Scripture to fit his *Mertonized* spirituality:

Progress in intimacy with God means progress toward
silence. "For God alone my soul waits in silence,"
declares the Psalmist (Psalm. 62:1).[44]

Does the word silence in this context mean silencing your
thoughts? Let me share the context of the version he quotes:

For God alone my soul waits in silence; from Him
comes my salvation. He only is my rock and my
salvation, my defense and my fortress; I shall not be
greatly moved. (Amplified)

It is believed that David wrote this either when Saul's son Ish-
Bosheth challenged him for the throne or during the time of Absalom's
rebellion. In either case, it is clear that during this time of duress he
writes about seeking solace in the Lord. He is asking for the Lord to
rescue him. He leaned upon the Lord during this time for he knows
that God is the Rock, the solid ground of our salvation. This biblical reference has no relation to David silencing his mind.

Psalm 46:10 is another passage often used to defend contemplative prayer, "Be still, and know that I am God." Below is the
entire line in context:

He makes wars cease to the end of the earth; He
breaks the bow and cuts the spear in two;
He burns the chariot in the fire. Be still, and know that I
am God; I will be exalted among the nations, I will be
exalted in the earth! The LORD of hosts is with us; The
God of Jacob is our refuge. Selah. (Psalm 46: 9-11)

It is obvious that the phrase "be still" does not mean to still or
quiet your mind by using a mantra. It simply means what it says—be
patient and know that God is in charge. In other words, *don't worry.*

The word silent or silence is often quoted by the contemplatives to infer that contemplative prayer is supported in Scripture.
In the *New King James Version* of the Bible the word "silent" is used
46 times. The word "silence" is used 24 times. However, not one

of those instances refers to any mind-silencing practice. I can give other examples, but Scripture clearly offers no support or description for contemplative prayer, and the contemplatives know it. By taking Scripture out of context, it is an admission on their part that the evidence isn't there. If contemplative prayer were scriptural, it would be described in such a fashion as to make no mistake about it. It isn't. On the contrary, there is a scriptural reference that clearly condemns the practice.

Meaningless Mantras—Vain Repetitions

While it is absolutely certain no reference can be found anywhere in Scripture that supports the practice of mantra-style contemplative prayer, there *is* a reference that actually condemns it, and it is Jesus Christ who says it:

> And when you pray, do not use vain repetitions as the heathen do. For they think that they will be heard for their many words. Therefore do not be like them. For your Father knows the things you have need of before you ask Him. (Matthew 6:7-8)

In order to really understand what Jesus meant when He said, "vain repetitions," let's take a look at the Greek language, in which the original words were penned. The Greek meaning for "vain" is futile, folly, and fruitless. Many translations render the word as "meaningless." In Greek, the word "repetition" means to stammer, stutter, babble, or prattle (like a baby); it suggests the idea of repeating the same words or sounds over and over in a meaningless fashion. It is interesting, and I believe significant, to note how these two words reinforce each other with the idea of meaningless stammering or unmindful repetition of words.

When both of these words are combined, as Jesus intended them to be, they do not condemn our bringing petitions repeatedly to God, but rather they condemn a mindless, meaningless repetition of words or sounds. And yet how many times do we hear the contemplative advocates telling us to do the very thing that Jesus here has told us not to:

I meditated for hours on words, images, and sounds. I reached the point of being able to achieve alpha brain patterns.[45]—**Mike Perschon, freelance writer for Youth Specialties**

The third phase of contemplative prayer ... a supernatural trance state[46]—**Charisma magazine**

The quiet repetition of a single word can help us to descend with the mind into the heart.[47]—**Henri Nouwen**

[T]he first step in faith is to stop thinking about God at the time of prayer.... Choose a single, sacred word ...repeat the sacred word inwardly, slowly, and often.[48]—**Brennan Manning**

Do not reflect on the meaning of the word; thinking and reflecting must cease, as all mystical writers insist.[49]
—**Willigis Jager, German Benedictine and Zen Master**

Jesus told us not to use vain repetitions as ... *the heathen do.* While it is certainly true the Desert Fathers experimented with contemplative prayer, what is not true is that it originated with them. In actuality, mantra meditation was practiced by pagan religions (including Hinduism and Buddhism), centuries before Christ was born. So it would only make sense that Jesus knew about this form of prayer and may very well have been referring to it directly.

Jesus tells us the heathen who pray this way do so because they think this type of prayer will more likely be heard and responded to. He then tells us not to be like them because our Heavenly Father already knows what we need before we even ask Him. In other words, the whole idea that God will hear us for our many words is rather insulting to God, if not even blasphemous, because it suggests that God is hard of hearing. Jesus says that, on the contrary, God is a step ahead of us and knows our requests before we even ask the first time.

Is the Lord telling us not to pray continuously or repeatedly for our needs and requests? No. In view of His telling us not to pray to

Him with meaningless repetitive chatter, contrast this with what Jesus referred to as *knocking* in Matthew 7:7 and Luke 11:9. In Luke 11, Jesus illustrates the value of persistence in prayer by telling the parable of a man who knocked at a door at midnight until his friend answered. He then explains the value of persisting in prayer as a practice of consistent and intelligent communication with God.

After Jesus tells us not to pray in mindless, meaningless mantras, which are nothing but an insult to Him, He tells us how *to* pray. He begins that instruction with, "Our Father in heaven, Hallowed be Your Name...." Prayer is an intelligent conversation between a loving Creator, who is a personal God, and His children. Jesus said it, and that should settle it for the believer.

The contemplative believes God has all sorts of revelations He is waiting to share with us, but our western rational minds are not trained to hear them. God is trying to communicate with us, but He can't because we do not become receptive until after the requisite number of repetitions have quieted our minds. Thus, the need to silence your brain through a repetitive practice or by focusing on an object to bring yourself into an altered state of consciousness.

Prayer is telling God about our needs and communicating to God, not trying to gain a personal revelation or mystical experience. In the biblical version of prayer we communicate to God and believe He hears. In pagan prayer there is a different agenda, a different understanding of God's nature, and thus a different technique.

Contemplative spirituality adopts the pagan technique even though a biblical understanding of God's nature as its proponents claim to have negates any reason for adopting the technique. What motivates them is a lust for secret knowledge that God has not revealed and a lust for a warm fuzzy feeling to indicate their intimacy with God. This is a failure of faith. They do not believe God has spoken once for all (Hebrews 1:1-2), and knowing Christ died for their sins and is seated at the right hand of God making intercession for them is not enough to convince them they are close to God. They seek a pagan experience to fill the *void* left by their deficient faith, thus the repetitive prayers, which are decidedly pagan. If they would obey Jesus' instructions in Matthew 6:7-8, then they would be forced to trust God rather than go by feelings and experiences; they would then be engaged in Christian rather than pagan prayer. Richard Foster continues explaining the reason for seeking the silence:

> The desert father Ammonas, a disciple of Saint Anthony, writes, "I have shown you the power of *silence*, how thoroughly it heals and how fully pleasing it is to God… Know that it is by *silence* that the saints grew, that it was because of *silence* that the power of God dwelt in them, because of *silence* that the mysteries of God were known to them." It is this recreating silence to which we are called in Contemplative Prayer. (emphasis mine)[50]

However, Ammonas, whom Richard Foster quotes, is wrong in his conclusions. It was not by silence the saints grew and not by silence the power of God dwelt in them but rather by God's Spirit. When Foster quotes Ammonas as saying "because of silence that the mysteries of God were known to them," he has revealed the underlying layer of contemplative prayer. The attraction to contemplative prayer lies in the secrets that are not revealed in Scripture but are supposedly revealed in the "silence." The voice conjured in the mind by vain repetition is said to reveal the secrets that the non-contemplative Christians aren't privy to.* But I ask then: Has God orchestrated a different class of Christians, *the upper contemplatives* who get the inside scoop while the rest of us wallow in the darkness with only God's Word revealed to us in the Bible?

Do We Need Contemplative Prayer?

Recently, I was invited to speak at a church that endorses contemplative prayer. I was curious as to why they wanted me there given my known position. The rest of the speakers in the other workshops were all teaching contemplative. I was the only

---

*Keep in mind that the word *occult* means *concealed* or *hidden* and refers to a branch of spirituality that seeks to uncover the hidden secrets of God and the spiritual realm. It stands in contradiction to the revealed Word of God (i.e., the Bible).

one teaching against it.

The pastor of the church sat in the back of the room and wrote down everything I said. I later learned that he invited me to speak so he could refute everything I described. He told his congregation in a letter following the workshop that I had confused the issue. In the letter, he said:

> After affirming the distinction between biblical contemplation and contemplation in Eastern mysticism, Brian Flynn then treated every occurrence of the phrase *contemplative prayer* as referring to Eastern mysticism. The word *contemplative* is not the issue; the definition of the word is the issue.

His insinuation is that there is a good contemplative prayer and a bad one. This is the issue they confuse. Virtually every occurrence of the term "contemplative prayer" by modern day contemplative authors *is* referring to Eastern mysticism. The definition of the word *contemplative* as described by Foster, Manning, Merton, and many others *is* Eastern. And in truth, there is no such thing as biblically-based *contemplative prayer*. It doesn't exist. To contemplate God's Word is perfectly acceptable and needful, but what contemplative advocates refer to is not.

Remember Richard Foster's warning I spoke of earlier in this chapter when he stated how practicing contemplative prayer could put the practitioner at risk of influence by spiritual beings who may not be from God:

> I also want to give a word of precaution.... I want to encourage you to learn and practice prayers of protection.[51]

If Foster is teaching the *good* contemplative prayer, then why does he warn his readers that they may be opening themselves to ic influence when they engage in it? And isn't it highly pre- ous to assume that, while in that realm of altered consciousness, the recipients will be able to discern good from evil? May I suggest that deception has brought them into that realm in the first place? In actuality, there is no difference between Eastern mystical Transcendental Meditation and Richard Foster's contemplative prayer. And they are both equally dangerous.

People who defend the practice of contemplative prayer do so because they love the euphoric feeling they experience while in the silence; and pastors love the number of new people flooding into the Church to get that feeling.

As a former practitioner of TM, I know that feeling; it is very empowering and seductive. After my psychic meditations, I felt tremendously euphoric. What makes contemplative prayer so dangerous is that Christian practitioners believe this power and euphoria come from God. And they believe the voice they hear is the voice of God. They are mistaken, and Scripture clearly warns us that just because something appears *good*, does not necessarily mean it is:

> For Satan himself transforms himself into an angel of light. Therefore it is no great thing if his ministers also transform themselves into ministers of righteousness. (II Corinthians 11:14-15)

Intimacy with God

Will contemplative prayer give the Christian believer communion and intimacy with God? The answer to that question is a resounding, *no*. On the contrary, engaging in contemplative prayer will break the sweet communion that is available to every born-again believer.

Why do so many feel the need to engage in contemplative prayer? At a local church, a contemplative-prayer advocate gave a seminar. He started his meeting by asking the questions, "Are you too often feeling distant from God? Do you have the feeling that your spiritual life has gone dry?" Many in the room nodded their heads *yes* to those questions. However, if *I* were to answer that question, the answer would be *no*. I feel very satisfied with my relationship with Christ, and I feel completely fulfilled in my faith. Why?

Recently, I had a debate on a local Christian radio talk show with Catholic priest Thomas Ryan, who advocates the need to combine Yoga meditation with Christianity. Shocked by his admission, I argued that Christians will find no answers in the methods and religions of pagans that send followers to Hell. If something is missing in a believer's walk with Christ, why borrow from *them*?

I told Ryan I found satisfaction in the Lord by reading and meditating on God's Word, through prayer, and fellowship with other Christians. He responded by saying, "Brian, I am so glad to hear that, and I am happy you feel so satisfied in your walk with the Lord, but many don't have that." He continued his advocacy for his Buddhist solution.

This satisfaction I spoke of with Ryan has come about as I have surrendered every aspect of my life to God. During those times when I held back from that total surrender, fighting with Him over which parts of my life He could take charge of and which parts He couldn't, discontentment and spiritual lethargy set in.

Often I struggled with relationships in my life, my finances, and my career direction. Time after time I gave my struggles and my problems to the Lord only to take them back a short time later. Each time He allowed me to have it back only for me to fail again and again. With each failure came a lesson that I could not do it alone. However, each portion of my life that I truly gave to Him, He picked up that area and made it something worthwhile and blessed. Over time, God has demonstrated to me that He can guide my life better than I can.

Too many describe the Christian life as tepid, while mustering up nothing more than a lukewarm enthusiasm for Christ. Many feel God hasn't come through for them and won't until they *do* something. Again we try to control God by making something happen and by earning points with Him. We desire an experience, and since God isn't *doing* anything, we initiate it ourselves. Rather than giving up control and letting God do the work in our lives, we come up with man-centered, man-prompted ideas and methods. Brennan Manning calls it "grabbing *a holt* of God."

Are we unwilling to completely let go and let God? Then we will never find that true, lasting satisfaction in our Christian lives. All the meditations, all the self-help Christian books, all the lighting of candles are not going to make any lasting difference.

Contemplative spirituality is nothing more than an attempt to fill that void with a man-made solution. In essence, they are attempting to build a spiritual *tower of Babel*. And as with all things man-made, it pales in comparison to what God can do.

If contemplative prayer or other Eastern practices were sanctioned or blessed by the God of the Bible, why are there no stories of any Hindus or Buddhists coming to Christ by these methods? Instead, we hear of Christians receiving *revelations* during contemplative prayer that all paths lead to God and that God is in all. If those revelations were true, this would make the Cross unnecessary and, in effect, null and void.

Can you imagine a Hindu coming out of a deep meditative state and shouting, "I know the truth! I heard a voice in my head declaring Jesus Christ is Lord!" If God wanted us to reach Him through this method, all Hindus would be Christians by now. Why would a method that has never brought any person of an Eastern religion to the truth of Christ bring a Christian closer to Christ? It will not.

But there *is* a way we can draw closer and become intimate with God having a full assurance of faith by His sacrifice on the Cross:

> Therefore, brethren, having boldness to enter the Holiest by the blood of Jesus, by a new and living way which He consecrated for us, through the veil, that is, His flesh, and having a High Priest over the house of God, let us draw near with a true heart in full assurance of faith. (Hebrews 10: 19-22)

The Pursuit of Common Ground

[R]eality itself is one, an integral whole, just as the cosmos and nature are one.... The Hindu, the Buddhist, the Muslim, the Jew, the Jain, the Sikh, the Christian and the agnostic all belong to the same planetary environment ... It has to be accepted that we all share in the same system of reality, while our views on its nature may differ. It is essential for the future for all the religious traditions to recognize this underlying unity.[1]–**Wayne Teasdale**

As I walked into the sanctuary of a local Lutheran church[2] with a few friends of mine one Sunday evening, I realized we should have come a little earlier. The place was filling up quickly. The special guest speaker was Thomas Keating, a Catholic monk considered one of the main individuals responsible for introducing contemplative prayer into the mainstream. While I knew quite a bit about Thomas Keating's beliefs and teachings, I was not prepared that evening to hear the disturbing and haunting remarks made by this priest in an evangelical church.

The event was sponsored by the Minnesota Contemplative Outreach. Their newsletter states that over a recent twelve-month period, they have:

- Served over 44,000 people through 3000 programs.
- Supported over 120 Chapters in 30 countries.
- Reached 12,000 people through Centering Prayer Introductory programs.

In Keating's "Transforming the Heart of the World" brochure, he states, "Contemplative Outreach aims to transmit the experience of Divine Love to the global community." Keating began the evening's service by leading the more than 300 in attendance through a twenty-minute centering prayer meditation. When the meditation time ended Keating proceeded to share his views on contemplative prayer. He said that by practicing this mantra-style prayer on a regular basis, the practitioner can erase the causes that affect unwanted, negative behavior.

Quoting Sigmund Freud and espousing the philosophies of Carl Jung to support his views, Keating stated that our psychological unconsciousness drives our behavior based upon influences from childhood, which he said is what causes sin. He claimed that contemplative prayer can cleanse wounded people from repressed self-knowledge and childhood trauma. In a kind of out-with-the-bad and in-with-the-good mode, Keating said that contemplative prayer was the vehicle to wholeness. Not surprisingly he offered no scriptural references to back this.

From such remarks as "we are the fruit of thirteen and a half billion years of evolution" to "contemplation is the *heart and soul* of the Gospel" I shuddered to think that this man considered himself to be a spokesman for God. Yet, as I glanced around the room, sure that many others in the room would look as shocked as I know I must have looked, the majority of people sitting there that night smiled, gazed admiringly, and even laughed. I had to remind myself that I was not sitting in a New Age meeting but was actually in an evangelical church. The words apostasy and paradigm shift flashed across my mind. When Keating said, "God is not the fearful God in the Old Testament," I remembered the words of David the psalmist who said: "The fear of the Lord is the beginning of wisdom" (Psalm 111:10).

Keating described contemplative prayer this way:

> Contemplative prayer is the opening of mind and heart, our whole being, to God, the Ultimate Mystery, beyond thoughts, words, and emotions. It is a process of interior purification that leads, if we consent, to divine union.[3]

Divine union, according to Keating, means not simply that we have fellowship with the Father through Jesus Christ, which we do have, but that we actually share God's divinity. According to the Bible, Jesus has bridged the gap between man and God, but we remain human and not divine. Keating suggests that in the silence of contemplative prayer we actually get in touch with *our divinity*, thus divine union.

Christian theologian Robert Dabney describes the problem of unification this way:

> The Christian believer, after he or she has been indwelt by the Holy Spirit, is "still a separate person, a responsible free agent, and a man, not a God. The idea of a personal or substantial union would imply the deification of man, which is profane and unmeaning."[4]

Unity of Experience

Is the *Christian* contemplative prayer experience similar to Eastern transcendental meditation? In an article in *Newsweek* magazine, "Religion and the Brain," the author describes how our brain functions in relation to meditative spiritual experiences:

> Although the field is brand new and the answers only tentative, one thing is clear. Spiritual experiences are so consistent across cultures, across time and across faiths, ... that it "suggest[s] a common core."[5]

These studies go beyond the research by Herbert Benson mentioned earlier in this book where he proves that a repetitive process brings one into an altered state of consciousness. These researchers actually locate the brain waves that prove a real biologically-based event.

In *Why God Won't Go Away* written by Dr. Andrew Newberg of the University of Pennsylvania and the late Eugene d'Aquil, the authors use brain-imaging data they collected from Tibetan Buddhists who were in trance-like meditative states and from Franciscan nuns deep in contemplative prayer.

One of the Buddhist monks described his "moment of peak transcendence" (which he has practiced since he was fourteen) this way:

> A feeling of energy centered within me ... going out to infinite space and returning ... a relaxing of the dualistic mind.... I felt a deep and profound sense of connection to everything, recognizing that there never was a true separation at all.[6]

One Franciscan nun described her moments of *ecstasy*:

> I felt communion, peace, openness to experience ... [There was] an awareness and responsiveness to God's presence around me, and a feeling of centering, quieting, nothingness, [as well as] moments of fullness of the presence of God. [God was] permeating my being.[7]

Although the article suggests that the experiences are not really spiritual but merely a brain function brought about by a repetitive meditative process, they do conclude like Benson that the experiences are similar.

They describe the nun's experience this way:

> During her most intensely religious moments, when she felt a palpable sense of God's presence and an absorption of her self into his being, her brain displayed changes like those in the Tibetan Buddhist meditator.... The fact that spiritual contemplation affects brain activity gives the experience a reality that psychologists and neuroscientists had long denied it, and explains why people experience ineffable, transcendent events as equally real as seeing a wondrous sunset or stubbing their toes.[8]

Their conclusion of a similarity of experiences is correct, but their summation is wrong. The feelings that the Buddhists and the contemplatives share is the immersion into the same spiritual realm.

They think this realm is God, but I propose that this is not the realm of God but rather a demonic one, thus a realm that no Christian should ever enter.

Interspirituality

Wayne Teasdale was a lay monk who coined the term interspirituality, a uniting of the world's religions through common ground. In an article titled, "Mysticism as the Crossing of Ultimate Boundaries," he describes interspirituality as:

- A crossing-over boundaries that mysticism makes possible and concrete.

- The spiritual common ground which exists among the world's religions.[9]

The term means to break down the barriers that separate religions. Through what means does Teasdale believe this breaking down and merging of religions occurs? None other than mysticism (i.e., contemplative prayer):

All these religious traditions [Buddhism, Hinduism, Christianity, etc.] emerge out of mystical experience, and mystical experience means a direct knowledge of and relationship with the Divine, God, or boundless consciousness. One can almost say that the real religion of humankind isn't religion at all, but rather it is mystical spirituality.

All traditions emphasize the deep interiority of the contemplative vision.[10]

Is contemplative prayer more than just an individual experience for unity or communication with God? When Keating spoke about contemplative prayer he stated that we could achieve unity of knowledge, Oneness with God and Oneness of all man. He believes that if we are all practicing contemplative prayer we will create a unity of the cosmic consciousness of all people. According to Keating, it is through this process we can create world peace. This is the same theory that is espoused by the Maharishi Mahesh Yogi, the founder of Transcendental Meditation. He calls it the "Unified Field." The theory is that when all are meditating, a feeling of calmness or peace is transmitted to those around them. TM websites are filled with statistics showing that when a TMer group enters a city and meditates non-stop for 24-48 hours the crime rate drops during that same period.

Supporters of TM state:

> Regular experience of the unified field through Transcendental Meditation has been shown to dissolve deep-seated stress in the individual, bringing marked reductions in hypertension, stroke, heart disease, and other stress-related illness. When practiced collectively in groups, this same program has been shown to effectively reduce societal stress and tensions, causing associated reductions in crime and social violence, and an upsurge of peace and positivity throughout the population.[11]

Whether the crime rate falling is attributed to the Unified Field is open to interpretation, but the theory is the same—unity of man and world peace can be achieved through a shared meditative practice. According to the Maharishi world peace can be obtained through meditation:

> Now every government can achieve national invincibility and secure the safety and well-being of its citizens. Such a government will naturally gain the permanent support of its people—and thereby secure its own longevity and dignity as a stable, sovereign government.—Maharishi[12]

What exactly are the Mararishi's plans for global peace:

1. Immediately establish a group of at least 1,000 to 2,000 peace-creating experts (depending upon the size of the national population) trained in Maharishi's Unified Field-Based Approach to Defense to secure domestic tranquility, stability, and harmony within the nation.

2. Quickly expand this group to 8,000 peace-creating experts—the number required to create a powerful influence of peace and harmony on a global scale.[13]

Thomas Keating believes some great days may be coming to the Earth:

God may be preparing a great awakening for the world, if God can find enough people to cooperate in this mysterious plan.[14]

What is this plan he speaks of?

In the writings of the major contemplative leaders, there is a common thread—the belief that through the shared experience of meditation and entering the transcendent silence, the boundaries that separate the world's religions can be erased, which will in turn bring world peace.

Wayne Teasdale states:

Meditation itself is also fast becoming an immensely significant force for understanding in the dialogue between East and West. We have only to consider the fact that every year there is an important meeting, a practical relating of Christian and Buddhist techniques and insights on meditation, a conference that takes place in an atmosphere of mutual respect, openness, trust and profound sharing in depth at the Naropa Institute, [a Tibetan Buddhist center in Boulder, Colorado] in order to grasp the importance meditation has acquired in relations between the Asian and Western religions.[15]

Mystical Union

The goal to unify man through a shared mystical religious experience is becoming more crystal clear with every passing day. The Sufis of Islam have "Fana."[16] the Kabbalists (Jewish mystics) have "Amidah,"[17] the Buddhists and Hindus have TM. And now last but not least, the Christians have contemplative prayer. Through contemplative prayer, many evangelicals and post-modernists say we can join the *shared universal experience.*

Listen to a few comments by dedicated New Agers and mystics who affirm their belief that the mystical element unites all humanity:

> A highest common factor [is] ... the metaphysic that recognizes a divine Reality ... [linking] every religious tradition.[18]—**Aldous Huxley**

> I would like to explore what I call *interspirituality:* a crossing-over boundaries that mysticism makes possible and concrete.[19]—**Wayne Teasdale**

> This mystical stream [contemplative prayer] is the Western bridge to Far Eastern spirituality.[20]—**Tilden Edwards**

It is with great sadness and dismay I tell you now that this New Age mindset has spilled over and is now invading Christendom. Evangelical author and speaker Tony Campolo, in his book *Speaking My Mind,* affirms this union:

> [M]ysticism provides some hope for common ground between Christianity and Islam. Both religions have within their histories examples of ecstatic union with God, which seem at odds with their own spiritual traditions but have much in common with each other.[21]

Later he asks the question, "Could they [Islamic Sufis] have encountered the same God we do in our Christian mysticism?"[22] With various examples, Campolo paints a picture of interspirituality through mysticism. Referring to Muslim and Christian mystics, he even tells us that the Christian mystics, such as St. John of the Cross, were en-riched by the teachings of Sufi philosophers. In comparing St. Francis of Assisi with the founder of the Sufi movement, Campolo says:

> Both men sensed a sacred presence in everything and claimed to have experienced a mystical union with God.[23]

The obvious implication of Campolo's statement is that God can be reached through mystical experiences, regardless of one's religion and beliefs. This is common thinking among contemplatives who often state that contemplative prayer does indeed provide a bridge to Divinity. The Bible makes it clear there can be no access to God except through Jesus Christ, but these writers negate this central claim in Jesus' proclamation by their promotion of mystical union with God for all religions.

Alan Jones, an Episcopal priest and a member of The Living Spiritual Teachers Project[24] states is his book, *Reimagining Christianity:*

> Christ and Buddha are not antithetical. They are not at cross-purposes. Neither are they identical. The man on the cross and the princely contemplative are different images telling difference stories. But they are not at war. They can be in conversation. There is grace in both.[25]

He later states:

> Jesus *is* the Way to a new kind of life. Jesus and Buddha have this in common with all great spiritual teachers—to make human beings more conscious of themselves, to get more real.[26]

Embarrassed by the Cross

New Agers and postmodernist *Christians* are attempting to deny or obscure the unique person and work of Jesus so He can be considered the equivalent of Buddha and other *spiritual teachers*. Jesus Christ is God. Buddha was a man. Jesus is alive. Buddha is dead. Can they not tell the difference? Emerging church leader Brian McLaren further develops this attempt in his book, *A Generous Orthodoxy*:

> This is how I feel when I'm offered a choice between the roads of exclusivism (only confessing Christians go to heaven), universalism (everyone goes to heaven) and inclusivism (Christians go to heaven, plus at least some others). Each road takes you somewhere, to a place with some advantages and disadvantages, but none of them is the road of my missional calling: blessed in this life to be a blessing to everyone on earth.[27]

McLaren wishes to be a "blessing to everyone on earth," but I wonder how many of those, who are being *blessed* by him, will be deprived of hearing the *true gospel* of Jesus Christ and believing in Him.

Contemplatives, such as Brennan Manning, believe we cannot even have a close relationship with God without the mystical, contemplative element. Manning states, "Intimate knowledge of God only comes through centering prayer."[28] That would mean that without a mystical experience of going into an altered state of consciousness there is no chance at all of knowing God intimately. Apparently, for Manning these experiences are more trustworthy and effective than the Word of God.

Combine McLaren's and Campolo's teachings that God can be found in mystical experiences regardless of a person's actual beliefs, with Brennan Manning's idea that we cannot even know God closely without contemplative, and what do you get?—a new Christianity that excludes Jesus Christ as being the only way of salvation.

Jesus said: "I am the way, the truth, and the life. No one comes to the Father except through Me" (John 14:6). I view that statement as good news. It is the end of confusion. It is the end of ambiguity. It is the end of wishy-washy postmodernist ideas. It is simply good news! When I became a Christian it was a relief and a joy to finally know the truth about God, to know who He is, to understand His nature, and to know His will.

However, for these contemplatives, Jesus' claim seems to be a source of embarrassment. They believe that the *exclusivity* drives people away from Christianity. Are they ashamed of Jesus' exclusive claim for salvation? That appears to be the case. And yet, shouldn't Christians follow the example of Paul, who in the end lost his life because of his stand for Christ?

> For I am not ashamed of the gospel of Christ, for it is the power of God to salvation for everyone who believes, for the Jew first, and also for the Greek. (Romans 1:16)

Through their shame of the gospel, the contemplatives wish to erase what they see as Christianity's exclusive claim. *If only we could rid ourselves of doctrine, disagreement, and certainty then we can join with our brothers of the East and share our knowledge of God obtained through meditation.* Alan Jones states: "A 'doctrine' is not like a fact to be believed but rather a way of being in the world that is validated by experience."[29]

The New Age offers empty feel-good platitudes and subjective meditative experiences. Sadly the contemplatives offer much of the same. *That* is what they should be ashamed of.

Global Peace Through Meditation

In Warren Smith's excellent and stunning book, *Reinventing Jesus Christ*, Smith describes the plan of several influential and popular New Age leaders. One of those, Barbara Marx Hubbard, believes that a time is coming soon in which the world will experience world peace and unity. She believes this will come about through a Christ figure, one who incidentally has spoken to her. In her book, *The Revelation*, her *Christ* tells her that the Bible end time scenario of a disastrous Armageddon can be avoided but only on one condition—the majority of people must come together in unity and realize their oneness with each other and with God:

The alternative to Armageddon is the Planetary Pentecost. When a critical mass is in the upper room of consciousness on a planetary scale, each will hear from within, in their own language, the mighty words of God. All who are attuned will be radically empowered to be and do as Jesus did.[30]

New Age leader Benjamin Crème also agrees with this premise. In his book, *Reappearance of the Christ and the Masters of Wisdom* he states:

One day soon, men and women all over the world will gather around their radio and television sets to hear and see the Christ: to see His face, and to hear His words dropping silently into their minds–in their own language.[31]

Benjamin Crème and Barbara Marx Hubbard are not referring to the Christ in the gospel. Listen to some of the statements that Hubbard's *Christ* tells her:

The second purpose of these writings is to call for the completion of the good news concerning the transformation of the world.[32]

The church is the body of believers who are conscious of being me.[33]

I did not intend for you to deify me, but to deify yourselves.[34]

How do Hubbard, Crème, and others mentioned in Warren Smith's book think such unity will come about? Simply this— through meditation (i.e., contemplative prayer). When Wayne Teasdale said that mysticism provided the "cross-over" to unite all people, he couldn't have been more right.

As New Agers such as Barbara Marx Hubbard, Benjamin Crème, and Marianne Williamson race to accomplish their world peace through mass meditation and unity, how are Christian leaders and spokespersons responding? And in such responses are these influential Christians aligning themselves with this New Age peace plan, one that calls for people to unite through the common ground of meditation, visualization, and other mystical practices. Alan Jones, in his book *Reimagining Christianity* says this of such an occurrence:

> The great religions are beginning to listen to one another. Is there a great planetary story emerging that truly has room for "the others" and that treats the earth as sacred? Is the human race in labor with the new version of its purpose and destiny? Or is it the same old story of fear and conflict?[35]

In contrast to Jones' vision for world-wide unity, the Bible predicts chaos in the days before Christ's return:

> And you will hear of wars and rumors of wars. See that you are not troubled; for all these things must come to pass, but the end is not yet. For nation will rise against nation, and kingdom against kingdom. And there will be famines, pestilences, and earthquakes in various places. (Matthew 24:6-7)

All these things must come to pass! And yet it does tell us there will be a time when everyone is crying out for peace, believing that it is right at the threshold:

> For when they say, "Peace and safety!" then sudden destruction comes upon them, as labor pains upon a pregnant woman. And they shall not escape. (I Thessalonians 5:3)

Christian Leaders, Contemplative Prayer and World Peace

It is imperative to see the connections between contemplative prayer and this expectation of world peace by New Age leaders. It is equally important to understand that a growing movement among evangelical leaders is heading in the same direction. I find it extraordinary that those Christian leaders who are involved in this global peace process are also advocates of contemplative prayer. Below is just a sampling of quotations to show these connections:

Rick Warren

Meditation: Many Christians use "Breath Prayers" throughout their day. You choose a brief sentence, or a simple phrase that can be repeated to Jesus in one breath.[36]

Global Peace: My hope is for a new reformation in the Church and a new spiritual awakening throughout the world.[37]—Rick Warren in reference to his global P.E.A.C.E. Plan.

Ken Blanchard

Meditation: Buddha points to the path and invites us to begin our journey to enlightenment. I ... invite you to begin your journey to enlightened work.[38]

Global Peace: Ken [Blanchard] has signed on to help with the P.E.A.C.E. Plan. And he's going to be helping train us.[39]—Rick Warren

Tony Campolo

Meditation: Beyond these models of reconciliation, a theology of mysticism provides some hope for common ground between Christianity and Islam.[40]

Global Peace: [W]e are to work with Christ to ... bring about global peace.[41]

Please understand, that it's not the efforts to relieve world poverty and suffering that should alarm us. And of course, we should have an attitude of love and peace towards our fellow man. But rather, it is the concerted effort for global peace by those who see mysticism as an important and essential element to this peace, as actually the bridge to this world peace.

Do the contemplatives believe their ideas supersede the gospel? If any peace comes, it will be a false one, and it will be short lived. It will be Jesus Christ who establishes a lasting peace on earth when He returns. In Rick Warren's book, The Purpose Driven Life, he tells us the details of Jesus Christ's return "are none of your business," and we shouldn't try to figure out [biblical] prophecy.[42] Perhaps this mindset is keeping the millions of Christians who have read his book from understanding what the Bible does say about world peace.

Barbara Marx Hubbard describes a time when a communication method shared by many different faiths will allow all people to experience a "Planetary Pentecost." Hubbard says this "Pentecost" will unite humanity through the realization that all have Divinity within. Will mantra meditation be that method to bring about this supposed world unity? And if so, will certain Christian leaders who are going full steam ahead with their own global peace plans fall prey to Hubbard's global plan? Thomas Keating seems to believe we could be on the threshold of that day:

> God may be preparing a great awakening for the world, if he can find enough people to cooperate in his mysterious plan.[43]

In light of Keating's steady promotion of interspirituality via contemplative prayer, discerning believers must wake up and take notice. If Satan could create a communication method shared by many different faiths and make all of them believe that the voices they hear are of God, think of the opportunities for deception that could result. I fear that he has already created it through contemplative prayer, and he merely needs more participants.

While Thomas Keating's unwitting goal of a "great awakening" could bring in the needed numbers, if there is going to be such a great awakening based on mysticism rather than the gospel, it is going to be one of great deception.

> For false christs and false prophets will rise and show signs and wonders to deceive, if possible, even the elect. But take heed; see, I have told you all things beforehand. (Mark 13: 21-23)

New Church on the Horizon

> We have moved away from the notion of a personal creator God and toward the divine self ... we have wholly embraced the idea of *spiritual evolution* and its attendant idea of an ascending spiritual elite. This is a truly dangerous idea that has had horrific consequences.[1]—James A. Herrick

Twelve years have passed since Jesus Christ intercepted my life and gave me new birth. My life with the Lord has been one of tremendous joys and growth and at times of struggle and hardship. After my conversion, many Christians asked to hear my testimony. What started as a short explanation grew into a full-fledged seminar refuting the New Age, its philosophies, and its practices.

While my heart will always yearn to share the gospel with New Agers so they may find salvation, God has taken me in a direction I did not expect. As I have shared my testimony and the seminar over the past decade, He has given me a deep burden for my brothers and sisters in Christ, many who have become influenced by New Age thinking, and they don't even realize it has happened. I am now persuaded that God has directed me to inform and warn Christians about the subtle strategies of the New Age and what some are calling the new spirituality and even a new kind of Christianity. It is sometimes a shocking discovery when these believers realize just how much this anti-Christian belief system has infiltrated their lives, churches, and families; they are taken aback when they see how these concepts and practices completely undermine their very faith and the message of the Cross.

Until recently I did not have a concrete example of any New Age practice or teaching within the church other than the influence of pop culture. That changed after reading Ray Yungen's book, *A Time of Departing*, and the research which culminated afterwards. Approaching some local pastors about the subject, they seemed rather nonplussed, explaining to me that it was simply a practice of prayer by the monks in the early history of the church. In other words— nothing to worry about. At first, I accepted their opinion because they certainly had more years of study and experience than I.

"You Cannot Talk About This!"

For a while I tried to shove the nagging notion that something was amiss into the back closets of my mind. But something Ray Yungen said in his book haunted me:

> In the spiritual climate of today a unifying mystical prayer practice fits the paradigm necessary to unite the various world faiths. In Western civilization, this model is the contemplative prayer movement.... [T]his movement is on the slippery slope that will lead to ... apostasy. For this to happen, as the Bible says, there will be "seducing spirits" who design a spirituality very closely related to the truth. Every Christian must therefore discern whether or not the contemplative prayer movement is a deeper way of walking with God or a deception that is attempting to undermine the very gospel itself.[2]

Finally, the light came on and I knew he was right—I could not ignore it any longer. Delving into the books written by the contemplatives themselves and well-documented research papers, I became convinced beyond a shadow of a doubt that contemplative spirituality was and is a heretical practice. I took my discovery to the next level and began including it in my seminar—a natural response to an important discovery. However, this caused quite a stir. Pastors seemed offended when I challenged the well-known names of the contemplatives: Foster, Manning, Merton, and Nouwen. Some of them acted as if I had blasphemed the Lord Himself. Suddenly I was called divisive, a trouble-maker, and unloving.

At my home church (a large metropolitan church), the pastors insisted that if I was going to continue my seminar there, I was forbidden to name names, and in fact, the pastors did not even want me mentioning the practice of contemplative prayer. "That's odd," I thought. "If we aren't promoting contemplative prayer in this church, why stop me from warning believers?" But I honored their request. "After all," I told myself, "this church isn't teaching contemplative prayer; at least I can warn my congregation of other New Age practices they might run up against." I was relieved to know my own church was not involved in Richard Foster's or Brennan Manning's form of spirituality.

But then one day something strange took place. I learned that Ray Yungen's book, which had been purchased by our church bookstore, had suddenly been banned from the store. The reason I discovered later—the book named names. I felt a little alarmed at even the idea that the book was now *forbidden*. A few weeks later, on a Saturday afternoon, while teaching the seminar in one of the church's classrooms, someone came up at break and told me that directly across the hall another seminar was taking place with a guest speaker—an avid promoter of Richard Foster and contemplative prayer! I was shocked … and angry. Here *I* and other watchmen were being silenced to speak the truth, while contemplative prayer was being ushered into my church. I had naively believed the pastors when they said they just didn't want to name names because it was too divisive; in reality, they had far more sympathy and dealings with contemplative spirituality than I ever would have imagined. And it broke my heart to know it.

After that, I knew I had to name names. And I knew I had to warn my brothers and sisters about contemplative prayer. Within a few weeks, I was called into a *special* meeting. Those present were furious with me— explaining to me that the church's policy was to *never* name names. I had violated that policy, and the pastors insisted I comply.

But how could I in good conscience? To do so would be disobedience to God. How can one warn the flock of false teaching if the names of false teachers cannot be discussed and analyzed? By this standard, the Apostle Paul would have to be silenced. Paul had no hesitation in naming the names of Hymenaeus and Philetus (II Timothy 2:16,17). Scripture gives many other examples of men of God, true believers, who had to name names to effectively warn the church. Not naming names would be like a parent sending her child out to play in the yard and not warning him to stay out of the street because the cars passing drove very fast.

"I cannot keep silent about this," I told the pastors that day. "Richard Foster is teaching heresy. The premise of contemplative prayer is that all paths lead to God, thus completely negating the gospel message of salvation through Christ's atoning work alone. And by your refusal to examine closely these teachings, you are leading the flock into a dangerous place of heresy and deception." I respectfully told them I was compelled to share the truth—I would not be able to comply with their wishes. Thus, it became clear to everyone in the room that day that I no longer had a place in that church. My passion to protect Christians from the practices and lies I was taught in the New Age stood in the way. With much sadness and a feeling of deep loss, I drove away from the church I loved. Where once I had been accepted and received with open arms, I was now looked at by the leaders as a trouble-maker. I had been a voice in that church, a testimony of what the New Age really offers, of what it really entails. Now, my brothers and sisters would not be warned, and I feared that contemplative spirituality would race in and flood that church I once called home.

How *could* I ignore such blatant heretical practices within the walls of the church? I chose to violate *policy* rather than ignore the needs of my Christian brethren. For this deed, I was silenced. I have never been asked to speak at that church again, and some of my closest friends who attend there have begun to distance themselves from me because of my stand.

As I stated earlier, my initial reaction to *A Time of Departing* was tepid as I did not believe this practice could possibly be epidemic. At the time, I was unaware that not only was it being promoted in my own home town, it had spread throughout America's churches.

A New Kind of Christianity?

A new kind of Christian? Transforming your church? Emerging Christianity? These now popular terms suggest that Christianity is changing. A new kind of Christianity is on the horizon. While efforts to become more Christ-like should certainly be applauded, what appears to be taking place in many of these efforts, though perhaps well-intentioned, is anything but becoming more Christ-like. On the contrary, through concerted agendas to remove the offensiveness of the gospel in order to reach the unchurched, the very message of the Cross, the only message that can offer salvation, is being diluted, revised, and often tossed out altogether. And amazingly enough, in many of these movements there is a common denominator—contemplative spirituality. And I will go so far as to say, if contemplative prayer was cut out of these movements, they would be no different than anything else; indeed it is the mystical element that is drawing people like flies. Take a brief look at just a few of these present-day movements to see what I am talking about—

Willow Creek

Willow Creek Community Church in Illinois has produced a number of contemplative authors and leaders, while the Willow Creek website boasts of a "self-guided" "contemplative worship service." Ruth Haley Barton, mentioned earlier in this book, wrote the curriculum for teaching contemplative prayer at this church. More recently, she and John Ortberg, a former Willow Creek pastor, co-authored a book together.[3] In this book, the reader is instructed to practice lectio divina, described by the authors as a slow meditative practice dating back to ancient times. At the back of this book, a list of additional reading resources include contemplative promoters such as Tilden Edwards, Dallas Willard, and Richard Foster.

Both Barton and Ortberg are promoters of the contemplative prayer movement, and both are featured speakers for the very contemplative National Pastor's Convention, hosted by Youth Specialties. This annual pastor's convention teaches yoga workshops and gives participants opportunity to walk through a labyrinth and attend contemplative prayer sessions.

It is important to mention here that Willow Creek senior pastor, Bill Hybels, shares a speaking platform at the Willow Creek sponsored Leadership Summit conferences, with New Age sympathizer Ken Blanchard and Rick Warren. Recently Ken Blanchard endorsed a book called *In the Sphere of Silence*. Of the book he says:

> This book is a wonderful guide on how to enter the realm of silence and draw closer to God.

And yet the author of *In the Sphere of Silence*, Vijay Eswaran, promotes meditation and its link to all religions:

> The Sphere of Silence, if it is practiced properly, is a very powerful tool. It is not just oriented to any one religion, it is universally accepted and practiced by almost all faiths on the planet. It is through silence that you find your inner being.[4]

One cannot help wonder if Ken Blanchard's and Willow Creek's love for Eastern meditation is shared by Rick Warren.

Rick Warren and Contemplative Spirituality

While Rick Warren, pastor of Saddleback Church in California, not only endorses the writings of Richard Foster and Brennan Manning on his pastors.com website and has included Ken Blanchard in his global peace plans, he also advocates breath prayer in his book, *The Purpose Driven Life*:

> The Bible tells us how to *"pray all the time."* How is it possible to do this? One way is to use "breath prayers" throughout the day, as many Christians have done for centuries. You choose a brief sentence or a simple phrase that can be repeated to Jesus in one breath.... Practicing the presence of God is a skill, a habit you can develop....

At first you will need to create reminders to regularly bring your thoughts back to the awareness that God is with you in that moment. Begin by placing visual reminders around you.… Benedictine monks use the hourly chimes of a clock to remind them to pause and pray "the hour prayer."… Sometimes you will sense God's presence; other times you won't.[5]

Some could argue that Rick Warren wasn't referring to mystical breath prayers in which a word or phrase is repeated. And yet, just a few paragraphs before his description of breath prayers, Warren introduces Brother Lawrence, a seventeenth century monk who practiced contemplative prayer. Warren describes Brother Lawrence's ability to "practice his [God's] presence all the time."

Former Catholic priest, Richard Bennett, says this of the monk:

Brother Lawrence was not only traditionally Roman Catholic but also disseminated teachings that have similarities with Hinduism in the *Bhagavad-Gita*, and with many New Age writers.[6]

Breath prayer, in nearly every case, is used or described as a technique to silence the mind or supposedly to "practice the presence." Richard Foster also advocates breath prayers as a method to achieve the same purpose. Remember it is repetition that brings one into an altered state of consciousness. Breath prayers are just another way of using meaningless repetition to gain an altered state. The practitioners believe they will feel closer to God through this method.

The medieval monks had a serious problem of trying manmade techniques to get closer to God. This is a failure of faith. We have a great High Priest and a throne of grace through which we can draw near to God. This was obviously not enough for them so they created such mantras of which the Bible never approves.

The same is true of "practicing the presence." This is a technique to convince oneself that he or she is close to God all the time when in fact again, we are to have faith in the finished work of Christ. What do we do if we do not "feel" close to God? Answer, believe that Jesus has entered once for all into the very presence of God for us and ever lives to make intercession for us:

> [W]e might have strong consolation, who have fled
> for refuge to lay hold of the hope set before us. This
> hope we have as an anchor of the soul, both sure and
> steadfast, and which enters the Presence behind the
> veil, where the forerunner has entered for us, even
> Jesus, having become High Priest forever according
> to the order of Melchizedek. (Hebrews 6:18-20)

The "practicing the presence" teaching is a man-made alternative to what the Bible says in the passage above. Here is the problem with the whole premise: It really does not matter if I "feel" close to God. Because if I am not close to God through the finished work of Christ, I am worse off if I simply "feel" close to God—my delusion would keep me from repenting and believing the gospel. On the other hand, if I have faith in the Word that says God has "reconciled us to Himself through Christ" (2 Cor. 5:18), then how I feel moment by moment is of little consequence in light of the unchanging reality of Christ, received by faith.

Therefore, practicing the presence, breath prayers and contemplative prayer are mere failures of faith in the true Gospel, or ignorance of it, leading to delusion.

Thousands of churches, pastors, youth pastors, and other church leaders participate in Purpose-Driven courses. If indeed contemplative prayer is being endorsed, promoted, and taught through Rick Warren, you can surmise that it will be coming to a church near you if it isn't there already, and the Purpose-Driven program will usher in contemplative prayer on an unprecedented scale.

On the Purpose Driven pastors.com website, Rick Warren's wife, Kay, tells readers about a book titled *In the Name of Jesus*, written by Henri Nouwen. She says, "it hits at the heart of the minister" and adds, "I highlighted almost every word."[5] And yet, in this book, an entire chapter is devoted to contemplative prayer.

In that chapter, Nouwen says this of the mystical prayer practice:

> Through the discipline of contemplative prayer, Christian leaders have to learn to listen to the voice of love ... For Christian leadership to be truly fruitful in the future, a movement from the moral to the mystical is required.[7]

If Rick Warren's global peace plans are carried out, then the whole world will be introduced to mystical, mantra meditation. For those of you who find these words seemingly sensational, let me ask you this: If Rick Warren is not a promoter of the contemplative prayer movement and all that this movement entails, why was he a featured speaker at the 2004 National Pastor's Convention which offered labyrinths, contemplative prayer sessions, and yoga? And why, in 2005, did Rick Warren invite contemplative leaders from Youth Specialties to give training at his Purpose Driven Youth Ministry conferences? These are questions that need to be answered.

Brian McLaren and The Emerging Church

A movement that has surfaced in Christian America is the emerging church movement. Leaders of this movement hold a position that the present modern church format does not attract today's postmodern youth. The style of these emerging church services might be best described as *candles, couches,* and *coffee,* in an atmosphere that is darkened and relaxed. The music is soft and somber, and attendance is primarily by those under 35. Is there anything wrong with creating this type of atmosphere? No, not in and of itself. However, atmosphere is not what we should be concerned about, but rather, what is being taught.

It is certainly understandable if a pastor or church wishes to create an atmosphere that will bring more people to the place of worship. After all, setting up a church in an abandoned parking lot, with only a tarp to stand under during the middle of winter would probably result in some pretty low numbers. But would it prevent someone from becoming a Christian in that situation? Not if the Word of God is being taught!

For the most part, the leaders of the emerging church movement believe that unless one has an *experience* at church, it is unlikely he or she will become a believer in Christ. What is the experience they advocate? The silence, brought about through contemplative prayer. On virtually every emerging church website I have seen and every emerging church book I have read, a full contemplative menu of mantra meditation, labyrinths, the silence, books by authors such as Thomas Merton, Henri Nouwen, Richard Foster, and so on, is offered.

Brian McLaren is considered by many to be one of the main leaders in the emerging church movement. According to a recent *Time* magazine feature article, Brian McLaren was listed as one of the 25 most influential evangelical leaders in America today. So the question we must ask is this: Is this leader of the emerging church helping the movement go in a contemplative way? The answer can be found in evidence that stands on its own.

In a 2004 *Christianity Today* article, "The Emergent Mystique," the author says that Brian McLaren sees Dallas Willard and Richard Foster "with their emphasis on spiritual disciplines, as key mentors for the emerging church."[8]

In light of other authors that Brian McLaren heartily endorses, it is really no wonder that he would esteem Richard Foster so highly. Of a book titled, *The Seeker's Way* written by Dave Fleming, McLaren has raving remarks about the book:

> I'm a huge fan of *all* Dave Fleming's work.... I'm especially enthusiastic about *The Seekers' Way* because it presents an approach to spiritual life and growth that is accessible to everyone.[9]

What is this "approach" that Dave Fleming says is "accessible to everyone?" Is he referring to mysticism (i.e., contemplative prayer). Richard Foster said that anyone can practice contemplative prayer and reach God. It's an approach that isn't just for the believer. The unstated deduction for the discerning reader is that God *can be reached with or without Jesus Christ* through contemplative prayer.

Brian McLaren is "enthusiastic" about Dave Fleming's book because it offers a spirituality that is "accessible to everyone." Fleming's book is a compilation of about a half dozen authors, each writing his or her own chapter. One chapter is written by none other than the interspiritualist, Wayne Teasdale. Another is written by Alan Jones, Dean of Grace Cathedral in San Francisco and a member of the interfaith, New Age group The Living Spiritual Teachers Project. Others include Joan Chittister and Marcus Borg, also members of The Living Spiritual Teachers Project. To understand Dave Fleming's "approach" that is accessible to everyone, listen to a few comments by the authors who contributed to *The Seeker's Way*:

> I don't believe that what we can know of Jesus is confined by the New Testament.... There is no such thing as "what really happened."[10]—**Alan Jones**

> Shame, shame, shame on those who mask as good what in reality is simply a new kind of human way to make ourselves "like gods" when we were all taught that what we are really supposed to be are other Christs.[11]—**Joan Chittister**

> [T]he way of the cross, the way of Lao Tzu, the way of the Buddha, the way of Islam and the way of Judaism all speak of the same path.... All refer to the same transformation of self.[12]—**Marcus Borg**

What mystifies me is how Brian McLaren can endorse a book written by authors who can say such things and yet McLaren is considered evangelical and a leader of countless young people in the emerging church movement. McLaren also endorses Alan Jones' book, *Reimagining Christianity*. In this book, Jones makes no apology for his disdain in the doctrine of the Cross (penal substitution) but rather refers to it as a vile doctrine.[13] And yet, on the back cover of this book lies McLaren's glowing endorsement:

Alan Jones is a pioneer in reimagining a Christian faith that emerges from authentic spirituality. His work stimulates and encourages me deeply.[14]

In the book, Alan Jones says this of biblical Christianity:

I was brought up a fundamentalist, [people who believe the Bible is the true word of God] but it never took hold. God's generosity kept breaking in. I couldn't stomach the exclusive interpretation of Scripture, and when I was younger this caused me a lot of distress.[15]

Jones goes on to say that Christianity needs some work—"as a way of imagination rather than a set of dogmas." He tells of a community in Japan where a statue of Buddha sits. The Buddha holds a young *Jesus* on its lap:

The image of the child Jesus sitting on Buddha's lap appeals to me and captures the spirit of this book.[16]

So why does Brian McLaren endorse this book? Perhaps he too cannot stomach the exclusiveness of Jesus Christ's message to mankind.

In his own book, *A Generous Orthodoxy*, McLaren states:

I must add, though, that I don't believe making disciples must equal making adherents to the Christian religion. It may be advisable in many (not all!) circumstances to help people become followers of Jesus and remain within their Buddhist, Hindu, or Jewish contexts.[17]

Such a statement would explain McLaren's subtitle for his book:

Why I Am a Missional, Evangelical, Post/Protestant, Liberal/ Conservative, Mystical/Poetic, Biblical, Charismatic/ Contemplative, Fundamentalist/Calvinist, Anabaptist/ Anglican, Methodist, Catholic, Green, Incarnational, Depressed-yet-Hopeful, Emergent, Unfinished Christian

Apparently, McLaren's belief system incorporates just about anything and everything and is certainly not confined to Scripture. Robert Reeves, Director of Communications for the Kentucky Baptist Convention, in speaking about Brian McLaren, gave an accurate paraphrase of McLaren's view of inclusiveness:

> [W]hile there is no assurance that there is salvation to be found outside of Jesus, Christians should not jump to the conclusion that Jesus is the only way to salvation.[18]

What is McLaren trying to say anyway? What could make Christians jump to the conclusion that Jesus is the only way? Could it be the words Jesus said? Or are we to assume that we who believe in Christ's deity have missed something in the Bible? Was there another way that we missed and McLaren found? Not a chance!

Interestingly, McLaren then backpedals when confronted on these statements. In an interview with Kentucky Baptists' newspaper, *The Western Recorder*, McLaren suggested the controversy was mainly a semantic one.

> I'm not saying I don't care if people are Christians or not … I'm saying I want people to be followers of Jesus, but to be a follower of Jesus in some situations may not require them to affiliate with the Christian religion.[19]

Huh? He goes on:

> This is a very well-known reality in missiology … Many Southern Baptist missionaries are building disciples in communities of disciples … that are meeting in homes or other places, but they are not affiliating with the Christian religion and disaffiliating with their own religion. This is especially the case in Muslim countries. They're affiliated as followers of Jesus but for a whole number of reasons, they are not saying, "I'm an affiliate of the Christian religion."[20]

"The issue," he states, "is that people confess Jesus as Lord. I'm interested in helping people actively be disciples of Jesus as Lord."[21] Which statement are we to believe? After months of writing, rewriting, and editing his book, he writes the first statement above. During all that time he was fine with the idea. Then when confronted he dances like a politician wanting to please both sides without actually having to take a position. Could it be that McLaren, like so many other contemplatives simply do not like Christ's exclusive claim?

In an interview in *Christianity Today*, McLaren states:

> I don't think we've got the gospel right yet. What does it mean to be "saved?" When I read the Bible, I don't see it meaning, "I'm going to heaven after I die." Before modern evangelicalism nobody accepted Jesus Christ as their personal Savior, or walked down an aisle, or said the sinner's prayer.[22]

Nobody? He may be right in terms of semantics but no one knew what it meant to be saved prior to the birth of modern evangelicalism? It sounds like McLaren is admitting he doesn't like what it means to be saved.

Unfortunately, Brian McLaren is another supporter of contemplative spirituality:

> They [Catholic contemplatives] believed no less fervently than charismatics that the risen Jesus is present in Spirit and can be experienced. But rather than locating that experience one step *beyond* the normal, they located it in the very *center* of normalcy. Instead of jumping and shouting, they typically recommended sitting in silence, walking calmly, or in some other way relaxing and quieting one's soul."[23]

> The charismatic/contemplative approach forms one spirituality in a way that enriches daily life. It can also prepare space in one's soul, I believe, for extraordinary

experiences of God—"favors of God" as medieval mystics would call them."[24]

I believe that the space he describes is actually a space they have given over to deception.

In an exchange with an advocate of the emerging church movement, I asked if there could be an emerging church movement without contemplative prayer. After dodging the question several times, he finally said no.

Does God care if we are in a postmodern period? Does not His Word stand the test of time? I do not believe that this generation or any generation requires a darkened atmosphere in church, or a silent experience in the spiritual realm through contemplative prayer, to come to Christ. The Word of God was powerful all on its own two thousand years ago—it is just as powerful today!

Many have come to Christ without ever attending a church. They have received Christ as their Savior in the deserts, on mountain tops, or in the jungles. What then is that common denominator that causes their conversion? It is the pure, unadulterated, untarnished gospel which is a living Word that pierces the soul.

If the emerging church advocates are looking for a more authentic vintage church to model, they are not going back far enough in time. Rather than reverting back to the time of the monastics, they should consider going back to the time of Christ. Rather than reading the books by Foster or Willard for guidance, they would be better served by reading the book of Acts.

In the emerging church services I have attended, a similar arrangement is followed: A darkened room, multiple lit candles, and stained glass images color the walls via projectors. Pictures relating to the evening's message are shown on the screen via PowerPoint software. The music is somber in tone but performed well. I admire the young people who put their hearts and efforts into these services. However, what is the message for the evening? Simply—don't be judgmental, and God is love. That is a fine message, but what is the primary reason that we gather? What is the reason for our belief? An atmosphere to attract young people is created, but sadly the gospel isn't proclaimed.

Recently, I attended an emergent church service where Brian McLaren was going to speak. The room was so crowded that some were sitting in the aisles. Those in attendance averaged in age from late teens to early twenties. While I marveled at the excitement and passion presented by the young people, I was utterly dismayed to hear McLaren's message. It could have been one given at any high school in America. Even the American Civil Liberties Union would not have objected. His message could have been summed up, "All you need is love." What a disappointment! Like other emergent church services I have attended, the gospel was never proclaimed at all.

Why go to such lengths to set up lighting, band, and staging yet never give the reason for our belief? With the opportunity McLaren has with these young people, if he had chosen to proclaim the gospel clearly and unambiguously, he may have had a major impact on those in attendance. They would have listened to him. Perhaps that evening the words of the gospel would have pierced their hearts and they would have become believers. He could have closed with an invitation to receive Christ and to accept Him as Lord and Savior. Unfortunately, this invitation was never offered. The reason he doesn't preach the gospel clearly is because as he says, "I don't think we've got the gospel right yet." How long must these young people wait Mr. McLaren?

What a mistake the emerging church movement is making by leaving out the gospel! I have considered what would have been my reaction to such a service if I were still a New Ager. I would have thought that there doesn't seem to be a difference between what I believe and what these Christians believe. *They share my belief that God is love and that I shouldn't be judgmental. Those Christians seem to be progressing in my direction,* I would have concluded. *However, what is the point of being one? I am fine where I am and have no need to know anything further about Jesus.*

In an attempt to reach the postmodernist, post-Christian culture, as they describe it, they actually end up affirming its false beliefs rather than refuting them and pointing to a better way—the only Way.

When the message is watered down, the uniqueness of the message of Christ is eliminated. Non-Christians may not like the gospel message but at least they will know the difference between their present beliefs and Christianity. As Scripture says: "For the message of the cross is foolishness to those who are perishing, but to us who are being saved it is the power of God" (I Corinthians 1:18).

Although the emergent church supporters see themselves as a brave cutting-edge movement, they are actually cowards when it comes to sharing the message of the Cross. However, I cannot blame them—they have been influenced by a timid leadership.

Paul gives this warning to the believers in Rome, "Now I urge you, brethren, keep your eye on those who cause dissensions and hindrances contrary to the teaching which you learned, and turn away from them. For such men are slaves, not of our Lord Christ but of their own appetites; and by their smooth and flattering speech they deceive the hearts of the unsuspecting" (Romans 16:17-18).

He later reiterates a similar point in his letter to believers in Philippi:

> For many walk, of whom I have told you often, and now tell you even weeping, that they are the enemies of the cross of Christ: whose end is destruction, whose god is their belly, and whose glory is in their shame— who set their mind on earthly things. (Philippians 3:18, 19)

The choice is clear—either embrace the shame of the Cross now and experience God's ultimate glory, or reject the shame of the Cross by glorifying in earthly appetites, and experience ultimate shame.*

If young people really want to shake things up in the church, following the dinosaurs of mysticism and liberal theology is the wrong choice. Being committed to expository teaching of God's word, and proclaiming the gospel every week, would be radical and cutting edge. It would also be far different from the purpose-driven-corporate-mega-churches that dominate

*Sermon by Pastor Bob Dewaay, Twin City Fellowship in May 2005

Christendom in America. My question to these young people is—do you have the courage to do it?

A Symptom of a Greater Problem

Contemplative prayer is not just a problem; it is a symptom. A *new* Christian church is rising, and it is sitting on a shaky foundation. This *new* church steers clear of all controversial subjects. Talk of Satan is not allowed while God's love is emphasized and His judgment de-emphasized. Discernment and testing of spirits are looked at as vulgar and divisive. The golden rule of this new church is, *accept all beliefs and do not criticize anyone, even a false teacher.* This is especially true if the false teacher has been endorsed by influential church leaders, many of whom have congregations whose memberships reach well into the thousands.

Why have church leaders refused to deal with contemplative spirituality? According to one pastor I spoke with, he had what he considered a solid reason:

> Our congregation likes it, and they feel a closer connection with God. When we offer the classes, the rooms are packed out. Contemplative prayer has brought in many people that normally wouldn't come to our church.[25]

If the right product is offered in this new church, people will sweep into the church like shoppers rushing to a day-after-Christmas sale at Wal-Mart. But we must ask ourselves, are we trying to save people through their *felt* needs? Are we to treat the unsaved as a demographic to analyze and market?

John MacArthur writes in his book, *Ashamed of the Gospel*:

> The philosophy that marries marketing technique with church growth theory is the result of bad theology. It assumes that if you package the gospel right, people will get saved…. The goal of market-driven ministry is an instantaneous human decision, rather than a radical transformation of the heart wrought by Almighty God

through the Holy Spirit's convicting work and the truth of His Word. An honest belief in the sovereignty of God in salvation would bring an end to a lot of the nonsense that is going on in the church.[26]

When the majority of church-going Christians are not taught biblical truth month after month and year after year, they become prey to false teachings. It is only by feeding on God's Word on a continual basis that we are protected from deception. Interestingly, most of the mail I receive comes from the laity. Much of the time, it is not pastors who are concerned and looking for answers—it is church members. Disturbed by the direction of their churches, these concerned members are challenging leadership, though they are often discouraged by their pastors from saying anything. They are told that they are overreacting. If they persist they are made to feel like agitators or troublemakers, made to feel unwelcome and eventually asked to leave. Many of these people write me, asking the same question: "Where do I go now? Where is there a church that will teach the Word of God every week? With tens of thousands of churches adopting the *new* church mentality, that is becoming a hard question to answer.

I once heard a well-known Christian radio host say that most pastors in this country had no courage to stand up for the truth. I don't want to believe that. I don't want to believe that Jeremiah 10:21 might be referring to these pastors, "For the shepherds have become dull-hearted, And have not sought the LORD; Therefore they shall not prosper, And all their flocks shall be scattered." Oh, what the church needs right now is pastors who will defend the gospel, no matter what.

Contemplative spirituality has waltzed into the church unopposed because market-driven principles and methods are taught at many of this nation's seminaries. Not only are seminaries failing to train prospective new pastors to preach the gospel and contend for the faith, but influential church leaders make the problem worse by *succeeding* at growing large churches without preaching the gospel.

Crumbling Arguments

In spite of the fact that a number of pastors asked me not to talk about contemplative prayer, insisting contemplative spirituality is from God, not one of them has ever been able to prove it through Scripture. And as of this writing, no one has even attempted to offer me a biblical refutation.

Proponents of contemplative prayer have two arguments: First they say other sources outside the Bible exist, which can be used to seek the truth; and second they insist that many contemplatives do not use mantras.

The first argument falls apart immediately with this simple question—How do we know that a source of information outside of the Bible is God-breathed? God has chosen to reveal everything He wishes us to know through His Word. I am not willing to bet my life on the words, ideas, or musings of man that are not supported by Scripture. Why would any Christian?

With regard to the second argument, let me illustrate:

I received an e-mail from a woman who attended a seminar on contemplative prayer—"No mention of a mantra was given to me at anytime," she insisted. She described her practice as sitting quietly, seeking the silence, and waiting on God's voice.

Let us accept her statement for the moment and apply the practice as she describes. I am to sit idly, close my eyes and silence my mind from any thoughts. I have tried to do this and find it impossible. How does one silence all thoughts? How does one stop thinking?

Many years ago, I sat waiting for the bus to take me to work on a dark, chilly Minnesota morning. It was just 5:30 am and not even the morning traffic had interrupted the stillness of the night.

I sat quietly with my eyes closed allowing my mind to wander. My thoughts criss-crossed from my job, to music, to politics, to whatever notion swept through my consciousness. However, I never let myself fall asleep, as I would miss my bus. What is the difference between this moment of silence and contemplative prayer without a mantra *or* a practice of concentrating on one's breathing?

Without a method other than being silent, how does one silence the mind? What the contemplatives discovered is the same thing I discovered, *you cannot silence your mind enough without a repetitive practice.* This repetitive prayer practice is nothing more than a self-hypnotic technique used to induce an altered state of consciousness. If you are simply sitting there letting your mind wander, you will conclude that contemplative prayer does not work. I would propose that successful followers of contemplative prayer are engaging in a repetitive method and simply do not wish to admit it.

Richard Foster chooses his words carefully when trying to prescribe mantra meditation to his readers. Rather than come right out and tell it point blank, he often tells readers to read Thomas Merton, Tilden Edwards and many more who are blatant promoters and practitioners of contemplative prayer and pantheistic in their belief system.

However, as careful as Foster tries to be, his writings are not without clear instructions on repeating a word or phrase to eliminate distractions. Take a look at a few of his remarks:

> Christians ... have developed two fundamental expressions of Unceasing Prayer.... The first ... is usually called aspiratory prayer or breath prayer....
>
> The most famous of the breath prayers is the Jesus Prayer.
>
> It is also possible to discover your own individual breath prayer.
>
> Begin praying your breath prayer as often as possible.[27]
>
> [W]e should stop to reflect and to treasure the words, to turn them over and over in our minds, repeating them ...[28]
> —Joyce Huggett in Richard Foster's book, *Spiritual Classics*
>
> Thomas Merton has perhaps done more than any other twentieth-century figure to make the life of prayer widely known and understood ... His interest in

contemplation led him to investigate prayer forms in Eastern religion.... [His book, *What is Contemplation?*] is an excellent introduction to contemplative prayer *for everyone.*[29] (emphasis mine)

In *Celebration of Discipline,* Foster employs a method that addresses the problem of simply trying to erase all thoughts. Here he gives some instruction:

> Having seated yourself comfortably, slowly become conscious of your breathing. This will help you get in touch with your body and indicate to you the level of tension within. Inhale deeply, slowly tilting your head back as far as it will go. Then exhale, allowing your head slowly to come forward until your chin nearly rests on your chest. Do this for several moments, praying inwardly something like this: "Lord, I exhale my fear over my geometry exam, I inhale your peace. I exhale my spiritual apathy; I inhale Your light and life."[30]

This description sounds like a method to me, and methods are never neutral. Pastor Bob DeWaay, of Twin City Fellowship Church in Minneapolis, describes it this way:

> Methods are not neutral: either humans can come to the true God by any means that they see fit or God restricts the means by which we can come to Him. This was proven by the fact that various forms of divination are forbidden where divination is defined as any technique used to gain secret information that God has not chosen to reveal. If we could come by any means, then Tarot cards, Ouija boards, crystal balls, psychic powers, etc. could all legitimately be used to contact God. Since certain techniques are forbidden, then the claim that humans can come to God by any means whatsoever is unbiblical. Therefore, we conclude that God has restricted the means of coming to Him and worshipping Him.

Pastor DeWaay continues:

> Scripture alone determines the valid means of coming
> to God. Scripture reveals one obvious restriction: *"Jesus
> said to him, 'I am the way, and the truth, and the life; no one
> comes to the Father, but through Me'"* (John 14:6—NASB).
> The Bible not only reveals the only way to salvation,
> but it also provides the means of grace for living the
> Christian life. God does not leave this up to man's
> ingenuity. He has not left us to sift through the religious
> practices of the cultures of the world in order to
> choose which ones to *Christianize*. Those who do are
> modern day Jeroboams who will not grant to God the
> right to tell them how God will be worshipped.[31]

Why is this happening in our churches? Why are false teachers
gaining ground and expanding their false messages? Why are they
able to bring thousands of churches together under one roof of
apostasy with such ease? Has Scripture predicted such times as these?

> For the time will come when they will not endure sound
> doctrine, but according to their own desires, because
> they have itching ears, they will heap up for themselves
> teachers. (II Timothy 4:3)

Is this what is taking place? Does the church have itching ears?
Is the straight, plain gospel not enough anymore? These are questions that need answers, and they must be answered by all believers—from the pastors and church leaders all the way down to the
everyday church-going Christians. In a time when many leaders are
preaching a false gospel, God is looking for believers who will adhere to God's Word no matter what the consequences are.

The greatest and most pivotal moment in my life was the day
I received Jesus Christ as my Savior and Lord. That day my opposition to Christ and my misguided beliefs about Him ended. For
the first time I truly knew who I was and who the Father was. I
wept in shame for my transgressions but wept in joy for Christ's

forgiveness. For the first time in my life, the world made sense—
the road ahead became clear. If I followed the Son, the shadows
of darkness would fall behind me, and even in the most difficult
times, my life before could not even come close to comparing with
how it is now. As the late Keith Green so eloquently sang, *like
waking up from a long lost dream*, so too, I woke up.

Through the last twelve years, I have often faced opposition
from my New Age friends and associates. It is tough to stand for
truth when so many disparage or dismiss it. As Christians, we must
defend our faith from the ignorant on a daily basis. The prejudice
that we experience is so strong that at times it can be overwhelming.
However, the joy in knowing the truth of Christ outweighs all the
criticism and strife. I have never been afraid to defend my faith, as I
have relied upon the book that sustains me, the Holy Bible. All those
difficult experiences have strengthened my faith in God's Word. No
matter how strong the winds of change may sweep through the
church, God's Word stands unchangeable.

When I see the church changing before my eyes and following
practices that I left behind, I can only describe the feeling as one
of deep betrayal. Some of the very Christians who helped me to
see my wretchedness and need for God, who taught me that these
New Age Eastern practices were an anathema to God, have now
opened the door and let the world's ideas breeze in unopposed!
How can this be? These are my brothers and sisters. They should
be joining me in my opposition, but they are not. I cannot just
merely stand at the church door blocking these currents of change.
I will run full force against them. For many years I ran against the
wind of God's Spirit, opposing the truth revealed in the Word of
God. Today, I would rather be running against the wind of false
doctrine than be swept up in the fleeting emotions brought by
unbiblical practices.

My brothers and sisters in Christ, I wish to end with this affirma-
tion—you were right. I, as a New Ager, was wrong. Jesus Christ is
Lord. He is the way, He is the truth, and He is the life. And because of
His mercy and His great love, I now know and believe this with all of

my heart. I have been on both sides. I have lived in darkness and in the light. The right way is Jesus. Now let us follow and obey Him only, running the race set before us with endurance.

> Therefore we also, since we are surrounded by so great a cloud of witnesses, let us lay aside every weight, and the sin which so easily ensnares us, and let us run with endurance the race that is set before us, looking unto Jesus, the author and finisher of our faith, who for the joy that was set before Him endured the cross, despising the shame, and has sat down at the right hand of the throne of God. (Hebrews 12:1-2)

Endnotes

Chapter Three

1. Anthony Robbins, *Unlimited Power* (New York: Fawcett, First Ballentine Books Edition, 1987), p. 26.
2. Ibid, p. 315.
3. James Redfield, *The Celestine Prophesy* (New York: Warner Books, 1993).
4. Description on James Redfield's website (http://www.celestine vision.com/main.html).
5. Alan Atkisson, "Summary" (*New Age Journal*, August, 1994, http://deoxy.org/9insight.htm, accessed 1/2005).
6. James Redfield's website (http://www.celestinevision.com/main.html, accessed 1/2005).

Chapter Five

1. Dr. Donald A. Bierle, *Surprised by Faith* (Bend, OR.: Global Publishing Services, 2003), p. 30. Dr. Bierle's research brings together information from many sources, as cited in his compelling and helpful book.
2. Ibid, pp. 32, 33.
3. Ibid, p. 35.

Chapter Six

1. Peter Jones, *Spirit Wars, Pagan Revival in Christian America* (Enumclaw, WA.: Winepress Publishing, 1997), p. 223. 2. "Astrology," Microsoft® Encarta® Online Encyclopedia 2004 (Microsoft Corporation, http://encarta.msn.com/ encyclopedia_761552380/Astrology.html, accessed 1/2005).
3. *Webster's New World Dictionary* (Simon & Schuster, Inc. 1/1/ 1988, 1994, 1991, 1988).
4. John P. Newport, *The New Age Movement and The Biblical Worldview* (Grand Rapids, MI.: Wm B. Eerdmans Publishing Co., 1998), p. 11, citing Hank Hanegraaf, *New Age Religion*, p. 200.

5. Irish Theological Commission, *A New Age of the Spirit? A Catholic Response to the New Age Phenomenon* (Dublin: Veritas; 1994), excerpt from Chapter 4.

6. *The Columbia Encyclopedia*, (New York: Columbia University Press, Sixth Edition, 2001-2004).

7. Ernest Valea, *A Comparative Analysis of the Major World Religions From a Christian Perspective* (http://www.comparativereligion.com/reincarnation.html, accessed 6/2005).

8. Brad Scott, "Yoga: Exercise or Religion?" (*The Watchman Expositor*, Volume 18, No. 2, 200, http://www.watchman.org/na/yogareligion.htm, accessed 1/2005).

9. John P. Newport, op. cit., p. 359.

10. Ibid, p. 393.

11. Ray Yungen, *A Time of Departing* (Silverton, OR.: Lighthouse Trails Publishing, 2002), p. 90, citing William Rand, *Reiki: The Healing Touch* (Southfield, MI.: Vision Pub., 1991), p. 48.

12. Walter Martin, *The Kingdom of the Cults*, (Minneapolis, MN.: Bethany House), p. 337, citing Benjamin Crème, *The Reappearance of Christ and Masters of Wisdom* (London: Tara Press, 1980), pp. 110-111 (also see http://www.shareintl.org/archives/AgelessWisdom/aw_bcwhoisGod.htm, accessed 1/2005).

13. Shirley MacLaine, *Dancing in the Light* (New York: Bantam Books, 1985), p. 420.

14. J. D. Salinger, *Nine Stories* (New York: Little, Brown and Company, 1991), p. 288.

15. William Goldstein, "Life on the Astral Plane." (*Publishers Weekly*, March 18, 1983), p. 46, citing Shirley MacLaine.

Chapter Seven

1. Lee Penn and Tal Brooke, "Neale Donald Walsch: Conversations with Myself" (*SCP Journal*, Volume 26:4 -27:1, 2003), citing Neale Donald Walsch.

2. *Seattle Post-Intelligencer* (Seattle, WA.: 8/22/1997).

3. ABC 20/20, Bill Ritter, Hugh Downs, Barbara Walters (American Broadcasting Companies, Inc., 4/3/1998).

4. Kate Maver, "Oprah Winfrey and her Self–Help Saviors: Making

the New Age Normal" (*Christian Research Journal*, Volume 23/No. 4/ 2001, http://www.equip.org/free/DN403.htm, accessed 1/2005), p. 19.

Chapter Eight

1. Ron Rhodes, "The 'Oprah Effect,'" (*SCP Journal*, Volume 22:4-23:1, 1999), p. 30.

2. LaTonya Taylor, "The Church of O," (Christianity *Today*, April 1, 2002, Vol. 46, No. 4), p. 38.

3. Ron Rhodes, "The 'Oprah Effect,'" op. cit., p. 30.

4. Bruce Shelley, *Church History in Plain Language*, (Dallas, TX.: Word Publishing, 1982, 1995), pp. 100-102.

5. Ron Rhodes, "Marianne Williamson—America's Glitzy Guru to the Stars" (*SCP Journal*, Volume 22:4–23:1, 1999), p. 3, citing Marianne Williamson.

6. Phyliss Tickle, *Publishers Weekly*, March 4, 1996, Reed Business Information.

7. Helen Schucman, *A Course in Miracles* (Glen Ellen, CA.: Foundation for Inner Peace, 1985 edition), pp. 358, 359.

8. Notations from an article by Edward R. Hryczyk, Catholic Reason. citing Helen Schucman, *A Course in Miracles* (Glen Ellen, CA.: Foundation for Inner Peace, 1975, 1985).

9. Ron Rhodes, "Marianne Williamson—America's Glitzy Guru to the Stars," op. cit., p. 32, citing Marianne Williamson, *A Return to Love* (New York: Harper Collins, 1992, 1996).

10. Ron Rhodes, "The New Age Christ of David Spangler" (*SCP Journal*, Volume 23:2-23:3, 1999), p. 21, referring to David Spangler, *Reflections on the Christ* (Forres, Scotland: Findhorn Publications. 1981), p. 10.

11. Ron Rhodes, "Marianne Williamson—America's Glitzy Guru to the Stars," op. cit., p. 32.

12. Marianne Williamson, "Interview," (*In Touch Magazine*, http://www.intouchmag.com, accessed 1/2005).

13. Neale Donald Walsch, *Conversations With God: An Uncommon Dialogue Book 1* (New York: G. P. Putnam's Sons, First Hardcover Edition, 1996.), p. 1.

14. Ibid, p. 39.
15. Ibid, p. 61.
16. Neale Donald Walsch, *Conversations With God: An Uncommon Dialogue Book 2* (Charlottesville, VA.: Hampton Road Publishing Co., 1997), p. 42.
17. *Book 1*, op. cit., p. 8.
18. Ibid, p. 191.
19. Ibid, p. 192.
20. Ibid, p. 13.
21. Ibid, p. 51.
22. *Book 2*, op. cit., p. 74.
23. Lee Penn & Tal Brooke, citing Neale Donald Walsch and Dr. Brad Blanton, *Honest To God: A Change in Heart That Can Change The World* (Sparrowhawk Publishing, 2002), p. 195.
24. *Conversations (Book 1)*, op. cit., p. 59.
25. Ibid, p. 94.

Chapter Nine

1. Francis Schaeffer, *The God Who Is There* (Downers Grove, IL.: InterVarsity Press, 1968), p. 66.
2. Ray Yungen, *A Time of Departing*, op. cit., p. 48, citing Jacquelyn Small, *Awakening in Time* (New York: Bantam Books, 1991), p. 261.
3. Jan Johnson, *When the Soul Listens* (Harrisburg, PA.: NavPress, 1999), p. 16.
4. Saint Andrews Abbey (http://www.valyermo.com/ld-art.html, accessed 1/2005).
5. Mike Perschon, "Contemplative Prayer Practices," (*Youth Worker Magazine*, http://www.youthspecialties.com/articles/topics/spirituality/contemplative.php, accessed 11/29/2004, accessed 1/2005).
6. Ibid.
7. (http://www.ymsp.org/about/history.html, accessed 1/2005).
8. (http://www.ymsp.org/resources/practices/lectio_divina.html. accessed 1/2005).
9. Daniel Goleman, *The Meditative Mind* (Los Angeles, CA.: Jeremy P. Tarcher, 1988), p. 53.
10. Bruce Shelley, op. cit., p. 116.

11. Ibid, p. 119.
12. Ibid, pp. 121-123.
13. Ibid, p. 117.
14. Art Jester, "30 Years After His Death" (http://www.texnews.com/1998/religion/merton1212.html, 12/12/1998, accessed 1/2005).
15. Ray Yungen, op. cit., p. 62, citing William Shannon, *The Silent Lamp: The Thomas Merton Story* (New York, NY.:Crossroad Pub. Co., 1992), p. 276.
16. Ray Yungen, op. cit., p. 75, citing David Steindl-Rast, *Recollections of Thomas Merton's Last Days in the West,* (Monastic Studies, 7:10, 1969).
17. Wayne Teasdale, "Interreligious Dialogue Since Vatican II, The Monastic Contemplative Dimension" (*Spirituality Today,* Summer 1991, Vol.43, No. 2, found at http://www.spiritualitytoday.org/spir2day/91432teasdale.html, accessed 1/2005), pp. 119-133.
18. Ibid.
19. Alan Altany, "What was the Christian Monk looking to find in his Dialogue with Buddhism?" (The Thomas Merton Connection, http://www.hundredmountain.com/Pages/pageone_stuff/mertonpages_fall00/merton5_fall00.htmlFall, 2001, Issue: Spirit in Crisis, accessed 1/2005), citing Thomas Merton from *Asian Journal of Thomas Merton,* pp. 233-236.

Chapter Ten

1. Steve Turner interview with Matthew Fox, "Natural Mystic" (http://members.tripod.com/nineoclockservice/mattiefx.htm,1995, accessed 1/2005), citing quote given by Thomas Merton to Matthew Fox.
2. Richard Foster and Emilie Griffin, Spiritual Classics (San Francisco/CA.: Harper, 2000, First Edition), p. 17.
3. Ray Yungen, op. cit., pp. 60, 61, citing Thomas Merton, *Conjectures of a Guilty Bystander* (Garden City, New York: Doubleday, 1989), pp. 157-158.
4. Richard Foster and Emilie Griffin, *Spiritual Classics,* op. cit., p. 20.
5. Richard Foster, *Prayer: Finding the Heart's True Home* (San Francisco, CA.: Harper, 1992, First Edition) p. 157.
6. Ibid, p. 156.

7. Pastor Bob DeWaay, Twin City Fellowship, (Minneapolis, MN.: his response to the question: "Can we get closer to God?").

8. Richard Foster, *Celebration of Discipline* (New York: Harper & Row, 1978 Edition), pp. 27-28.

9. Ibid, p. 28 (in his footnotes of some editions).

10. Tilden Edwards, *Living in the Presence* (San Francisco, CA.: HarperCollins Paperback Edition, 1994), p. 18.

11. Richard Foster, *Celebration of Discipline*, 1978, op. cit., p. 22.

12. Spiritual Directors International (http://www.sdiworld.org).

13. A spiritual director is someone who directs a person who is practicing contemplative prayer as a means of *hearing* from God.

14. Agnieszka Tennant, "Drawing Closer to God" (*Today's Christian Woman*, September/October 2004, Vol. 26, No. 5), p. 14. Reprinted by permission from *Today's Christian Woman* magazine, published by *Christianity Today International*, Carol Stream, Illinois.

15. Chris Armstrong and Steve Gertz, "Got Your 'Spiritual Director' Yet?" (Christianity *Today*, May 2, 2003).

16. Richard Foster, *Celebration of Discipline*, 1978, op cit., p. 16.

17. Ruth Haley Barton, "Beyond Words," (*Discipleship Journal*, NavPress, Vol. 113, 1999), p. 35.

18. Ibid, p. 38.

19. Ruth Haley Barton, *Invitation to Solitude and Silence, Experiencing God's Transforming Presence* (Downers Grove, IL.: InterVarsity Press, 2004), pp. 40-42.

20. Ruth Haley Barton, op. cit., p. 138.

21. Richard Foster, *Celebration of Discipline*, op. cit., 1988 Revised Edition, p. 220.

22. Tilden Edwards, *Spiritual Friend* (New York: Paulist Press, 1980), p. 18.

23. Tilden Edwards, "Jesus and Buddha: Good Friends," (*Shalem Institute for Spiritual Formation*, http://www.shalem.org/sn/24.1te.html, Winter 2000, Volume xxiv, No. 1, accessed 1/2005).

24. Tilden Edwards, *Living in the Presence*, op. cit., pp. 18-19.

25. Brennan Manning, *The Gentle Revolutionaries* (Denville, NJ.: Dimension Books, 1976), pp. 103-104. He quotes from a book

by Father George A. Maloney, *The Breath of a Mystic*. All of Father
Maloney's books are listed on the back cover of Manning's book.

26. Oxford Dictionary of the Christian Church (Oxford
University Press, http://www.oxfordreference.com/pages/
Subjects_and_Titles__2E_R02, accessed 6/2005).

27. Brennan Manning, *Signature of Jesus* (Sisters, OR.: Multnomah
Publishers, Revised Edition, 1996), p. 188.

28. Ibid, pp. 211, 212.

29. Ibid, p. 212.

30. Ibid.

31. Ibid, p. 218.

32. Ibid.

33. Michael Persinger, *TM and Cult Mania* , U.S. District Court, NJ.,
E.J. Malnak vs. Maharishi Mahesh Yogi. (North Quincy, MA.:
The Christopher Publishing House, Sworn affidavit by G. J.
Randoff., 1980).

34. Michael Persinger, *TM and Cult Mania*, op. cit., p. 56.

35. Inner Explorations, "Questions About Centering Prayer"
(http://www.innerexplorations.com/chmystext/ques2.htm,
accessed 6/ 2005).

36. "What is kundalini energy?" (Kundalini Network, http://
home.wxs.nl/~eijl0000/par11.html, accessed 6/ 2005).

37. Kundalini - "Short Circuits and Risks and Information" (http:/ /
kundalini.se/eng/engkni_1024.html, accessed 6/ 2005).

38. Ibid.

39. Cassandrah Batya, "'The Great, Subtle Lie'" of Contemplative
Spirituality" (A Christian Journey, http://achristian
journey.blogs.com/achristianjourney/2005/04/the_ great _ subtl
.html, accessed 6/ 2005).

40. Ibid.

41. Steve Turner interview with Matthew Fox, "Natural Mystic?" op. cit.

42. Ray Yungen, *A Time of Departing*, op. cit., p. 39.

43. Ron Rhodes, "Anthony Robbins and the Quest for Unlimited
Power" (*SCP Journal*, Volume 22:2-22:3, 1998), citing Anthony
Robbins, *Awaken The Giant Within* , Free Press), pp. 217, 218, 219.

44. Richard Foster, *Prayer: Finding the Heart's True Home*, op. cit., p. 155.

45. Mike Perschon, "Desert Youth Worker Disciplines, Mystics, and
the Contemplative Life" (Youth Worker Journal, Nov/Dec 2004,
http://www.youthspecialties.com/articles/topics/spirituality/
desert.php, accessed 6/ 2005).

46. Jim Goll, "Be Still and Know" (*Charisma Magazine*, October 2004, http://www.charismamag.com/a.php?ArticleID=9723, accessed 6/ 2005).

47. Henri Nouwen, *The Way of the Heart* (San Francisco, CA: Harper, Reprint Edition 1991), p. 81.

48. Brennan Manning, *Signature of Jesus*, op. cit., pp. 212, 218.

49. Ray Yungen, *A Time of Departing*, op. cit., p. 38, citing Willigis Jager, *Contemplation: A Christian Path* (Triumph Books, 1994), p. 31.

50. Richard Foster, *Prayer: Finding the Heart's True Home*, op. cit., p. 155.

51. Ibid, p. 157.

Chapter 11

1. Wayne Teasdale, "The Meeting of East and West: Elements of a Relationship," (Spirituality *Today*, Summer 1986, Vol. 38, http://www.spiritualitytoday.org/spir2day/863822teasdale.html, accessed 6/2005).

2. Prince of Peace Lutheran Church Burnsville, MN April 10, 2005.

3. Thomas Keating, "Centering Prayer as Divine Therapy" (Reprinted from Trinity News: the Magazine of Trinity Church in the City of New York, 1995 Vol. 42, 4, p. 8-11, http://www.thecentering.org/therapy.html, accessed 6/ 2005).

4. Alan Morrison citing Robert Dabney (1820-1898) "The Evangelical Attraction to Mysticism" (Diakrisis Ministries, http://www.diakrisis.org/evanmyst.htm

5. Sharon Begley, "Religion and the Brain," (Newsweek, May 7, 2001, p. 53).

6. Ibid.

7. Ibid.

8. Ibid.

9. Wayne Teasdale, "Mysticism as the Crossing of Ultimate Boundaries: A Theological Reflection" (The Golden String Newsletter, http://www.bedegriffiths.com/golden/gs_10.htm, accessed 6/2005).

10. Ibid.

11. Scientific Foundation, "Creating Coherent National Consciousness: The 'Maharishi Effect'" (Achieving World Peace and National Invincibility, http://www.invincibility.org/maharishi _ effect .html, accessed 6/ 2005).

12. Ibid, quoting Maharishi (http://www.invincibility.org).

13. Ibid, (http://www.invincibility.org/action.html).

14. Thomas Keating, "Transforming the Heart of the World 20th Anniversary brochure" (Contemplative Outreach, Butler, New Jersey).

15. Wayne Teasdale, "The Meeting of East and West: Elements of a Relationship," op. cit.

16. *The Dictionary of Mysticism and the Occult* defines it as: "The Act of merging with the Divine Oneness." (Quoting Ray Yungen, *A Time of Departing*, op. cit., p. 62).

17. From Kabbalah Made Easy: "An indication that one need not be a mystic to meditate is a passage from the Code of Jewish Law regarding the daily prayer, called the "amidah," which is recited three times a day. This is the way the pious prayed, they would meditate and focus their minds on the prayers until they reached a state when physicality was nullified, and the intellect was strengthened until they reached a state close to rophecy.'" (http://www.kabbalahmadeeasy.com/prevarticles/meditation.html, accessed 6/ 2005).

18. Ron S. Miller and New Age Journal, *As Above, So Below* (New York: G. P. Putnam's Sons, 1992, p. 2, citing Aldous Huxley, *Perennial Philosophy*).

19. Wayne Teasdale, "Mysticism as the Crossing of Ultimate Boundaries: A Theological Reflection," op. cit.

20. Tilden Edwards, *Spiritual Friend* (New York: Paulist Press, 1980, pp. 162-163).

21. Tony Campolo, *Speaking My Mind* (Nashville, TN: W Publishing Group, Div. Thomas Nelson, 2004), p. 149.

22. Ibid, p. 150.

23. Ibid.

24. The Living Spiritual Teachers Project (http://www.spirituality health.com/newsh/items/blank/item_3635.html, members include Buddhist Monks, New Age Gurus, Zen Masters and so forth. They include: Marianne Williamson, Ram Dass, Andrew Harvey and Thich Nhat Hanh).

25. Alan Jones, *Reimagining Christianity* (Hoboken, NJ:John Wiley & Sons, 2005), pp. 146-147.

26. Ibid, p. 194.

27. Brian McLaren, *A Generous Orthodoxy*, (El Cajon, CA: Zondervan, 2004, p. 113).

28. Brennan Manning, *Gentle Revolutionaries*, p. 104, op. cit.

29. Alan Jones, *Reimagining Christianity*, pp. 207-208, op. cit.

30. Warren Smith, *Reinventing Jesus Christ* (Ravenna, OH: Conscience Press, 2002), p. 57.

31. Ibid, p. 30.

32. Ibid, p. 17.

33. Ibid.

34. Ibid, p. 18.
35. Alan Jones, *Reimagining Christianity*, pp. 232-233.
36. Rick Warren, from www.pastors.com website (http://www. pastors. com/RWMT/?id=71&artid=1960&expand=1, October 9, 2002, also see *The Purpose Driven Life*, Grand Rapids, MI: Zondervan, 2002), pp. 89, 299.
37. Dan Wooding citing Rick Warren, "Rick Warren Hits Home Run With Announcement of Global Peace Plan to Battle the Giants of Our World" (Assist Ministries, http:// www.ksgn.com/extras/saddleback.asp, accessed 6/ 2005).
38. Ken Blanchard and Frank Metcalf *What Would Buddha Do at Work?* (Berkeley, CA: Seastone, imprint of Ulysees Press, 2001), foreword.
39. Rick Warren in a November 2003 sermon at Saddleback where he introduced the global peace plan and announced that Ken Blanchard had signed on to help implement the plan. (to access sermon video clip: http://www.lighthousetrailsresearch.com/ pressreleasevideoclip.htm).
40. Tony Campolo, *Speaking My Mind*, p. 149, op. cit.
41. Tony Campolo, *Speaking My Mind*, p. 225, op. cit.
42. Rick Warren, *The Purpose Driven Life*, op. cit., pp. 285-286.
43. Thomas Keating, "Transforming the Heart of the World" (Contemplative Outreach, Ltd., http://www.centeringprayer. com/ Generosity/reachout.htm, accessed 6/ 2005).

Chapter 12

1. Interview with James Herrick regarding his book, *The Making of the New Spirituality* (Downers Grove, IL: InterVarsity Press, 2003, interview at http://www.gospelcom.net/ivpress/title/ int/2398.pdf, accessed 1/2005).
2. Ray Yungen, *A Time of Departing*, op. cit., p. 136.
3. Ruth Haley Barton and John Ortberg, *An Ordinary Day with Jesus Leader's Guide* (Grand Rapids, MI: Zondervan, 2001).
4. Vijay Eswaran, *In the Sphere of Silence* (Hong Kong: Rythm House, 2005, excerpt from website http:// www.inthesphereofsilence.com/desktop Default. aspx? Myurl =p_default &tabindex=3& tabid=11&subtabid=42, accessed 6/2005).

5. Rick Warren, *Purpose-Driven Life* (Grand Rapids, MI: Zondervan, 2002), p. 89. Also see p. 299.

6. Richard Bennett, "The Adulation of Man in The Purpose Driven Life" (Berean Beacon website, http://www.berean beacon.org/articles/rick_warren_purpose_driven.htm, accessed 6/2005).

7. Ray Yungen, *A Time of Departing* (Silverton, OR: Lighthouse Trails Publishing, 2002) p. 134, citing Henri Nouwen, *In the Name of Jesus* (New York: Crossroad, 1989), pp. 6, 31-32.

8. Andy Crouch, "The Emergent Mystique" (*Christianity Today*, November 2004, http://www.christianitytoday.com/ct/200401112.36.html, accessed 6/2005).

9. Brian McLaren speaking on Dave Fleming's book, *The Seeker's Way* (http://cleave.blogs.com/pomomusings/2005/01/dave_flemings_t.html, accessed 6/2005).

10. Alan Jones, *Reimagining Christianity* (Hoboken, NJ: John Wiley & Sons, Inc., 2005), p. 209.

11. Joan Chittister, "We have something to be ashamed of: but what is it?" (National Catholic Reporter, Vol. 2, No. 8, June 2, 2004, http://www.nationalcatholicreporter.org/fwis/fw060204.htm, accessed 6/2005).

12. Marcus Borg, *The Heart of Christianity* (New York: Harper Collins, paperback edition, 2004), p. 216.

13. Alan Jones, *Reimagining Christianity* (Hoboken, NJ: John Wiley & Sons, Inc., 2005), p. 167-168.

14. Brian McLaren endorsing back cover Alan Jones, *Reimagining Christianity*, op. cit.

15. Alan Jones, *Reimagining Christianity*, op. cit., preface.

16. Ibid, p. 12.

17. Brian McLaren, *A Generous Orthodoxy* (Grand Rapids, MI: Zondervan, 2004), p. 260.

18. Robert Reeves, "McLaren Withdrawn From Evangelism Conference Lineup" (Kentucky Baptist Convention, 2/2005, http://www.kybaptist.org/kbc/welcome.nsf/pages/mclaren, accessed 6/ 2005).

19. Trennis Henderson citing Brian McLaren, "McLaren speaks in Kentucky after controversy" (Associated Baptist Press, April 15, 2005, http://www.biblicalrecorder.org/content/

news/2005/4_15_2005/ne150405mclaren.shtml, accessed 6/ 2005).
20. Ibid.
21. Ibid.
22. Andy Crouch citing Brian McLaren "The Emergent Mystique" (*Christianity Today*, November 2004, http://www.christianity today. com /ct/200401112.36.html, accessed 6/2005).
23. Brian McLaren, *A Generous Orthodoxy*, op. cit., p. 176.
24. Ibid, p. 177.
25. Conversation between Brian Flynn and a pastor in Minneapolis in March 2004.
26. Nathan Busenitz, "The Gospel According to Hybels & Warren" Shepherds' Fellowship, 2003, http://www.biblebb.com/files/gath w.htm, accessed 1/2005), citing John MacArthur, *Ashamed of the Gospel* (Wheaton, IL: Crossway Books, 1993, electronic edition).
27. Richard Foster, *Prayer: Finding the Heart's True Home*, op. cit., pp. 122-123.
28. Richard Foster, Emilie Griffin, *Spiritual Classics*, op. cit., p. 12, citing Joyce Huggett.
29. Ibid, pp. 17, 21.
30. Richard Foster, *Celebration of Discipline*, 1978; op. cit., p. 25.
31. Bob DeWaay, ISSUE 83 - Contemporary Christian Divination July/August 2004 (http://www.twincityfellowship.com/cic/articles /issue83.htm).

Index

A

B

H

Hale-Bopp comet 109
Heaven's Gate Cult 109
Heaven and Earth 115
Herrick, James A. 193
higher self 46, 96
Hinduism
80, 84, 89, 90, 92, 93, 95, 106, 122, 139, 171, 177, 182, 199
Holy Spirit 110, 111, 149, 151, 161, 211
Hitler 127
Holy Spirit 110, 111, 149, 151, 161, 211
Hubbard, Barbara Marx 188, 189, 192
Human Potential Movement 96
Huxley, Aldous 185
Hymenaeus and Philetus 196
Hybels, Bill 198
hypnosis 133

I

imagination 97, 147
In the Name of Jesus 200
In the Sphere of Silence 198, 228
In Touch magazine 124
inclusivism 187
International Academy of Meditation 92
interspirituality 139, 182, 184, 185, 192
Invitation to Solitude and Silence 154, 156

J

Jager, Willigis 171
Jesus and Buddha: Good Friends 157
Jesus Christ 9, 17, 35, 49, 85, 86, 105, 109, 110, 112, 117, 120, 127, 138, 141, 157, 167, 193, 216, 217
Jesus Prayer 213
Jewish mystics 185
Johnson, Jan 133
Jones, Alan 186, 188, 190, 203, 204
Jones, Dr. Peter 86, 87
Joyce Huggett 214

V

vain repetitions 144, 170, 171
Van Praagh, James 114, 115
Vatican II 16, 139
vintage church 207

W

Walsch, Neale Donald 103, 107, 125, 126, 127, 128, 129
Warren, Kay   200
Warren, Rick 191, 192, 198, 199, 200, 201
What is Contemplation? 214
wicca 87, 90, 99
Willard, Dallas   197, 202
Williams, Paul 104
Williamson, Marianne 102, 103, 121, 123, 124, 189
Willow Creek Community Church 152, 197, 198
witchcraft 86, 87, 90, 99

Y

Yoga 90, 93, 95, 96, 159, 164, 165, 176, 198, 201
Youth Ministry & Spirituality Project   135
Youth Specialties 134, 135, 171, 197, 201
Youth Worker Journal   134
Yungen, Ray 8, 132, 168, 194, 195

Z

Zen 140, 143

To Order Additional copies of:

Running Against the Wind

send $12.95 plus $3.25 for shipping to:

Lighthouse Trails Publishing Company
P.O. Box 958
Silverton, Oregon 97381
www.lighthousetrails.com

You may also order by calling or faxing our
toll free number:
866/876-3910
[ORDER LINE]
or e-mail editor@lighthousetrails.com.

For all other calls, 503/873-9092.
For more information about contemplative spirituality:
www.lighthousetrailsresearch.com

Running Against the Wind and other books by Lighthouse
Trails Publishing are available through all major outlet stores,
bookstores, online bookstores and Christian bookstores.

Bookstores may order through Ingram, Spring Arbor or Faithworks.
Libraries may order through Baker and Taylor.

Special Quantity Discounts Available.
Also check out our website for special overseas ordering
through one of our overseas distributors.

You may correspond with Brian Flynn
by going to his web site at:
www.onetruthministries.com

Other Books By
Lighthouse Trails Publishing

A Time of Departing
by Ray Yungen

Laughter Calls Me
by Catherine Brown

Tapestry: The Journey of Laurel Lee
by Laurel Lee

For Many Shall Come in My Name
by Ray Yungen